D1090979

Reeducating Teachers for Cultural Awareness

Roger M. Baty

Published in cooperation with the Stanford International Development Education Center

The Praeger Special Studies program—utilizing the most modern and efficient book production techniques and a selective worldwide distribution network—makes available to the academic, government, and business communities significant, timely research in U.S. and international economic, social, and political development.

Reeducating Teachers for Cultural Awareness

Preparation for Educating Mexican–American Children in Northern California

PRAEGER SPECIAL STUDIES IN U.S. ECONOMIC AND SOCIAL DEVELOPMENT

Praeger Publishers New York Washington London

PRAEGER PUBLISHERS
111 Fourth Avenue, New York, N.Y. 10003, U.S.A.
5, Cromwell Place, London S.W.7, England

Published in the United States of America in 1972
by Praeger Publishers, Inc.

Library of Congress Catalog Card Number: 75-173278

Printed in the United States of America

This work was developed under a contract/grant
with the U.S. Office of Education, Department of
Health, Education and Welfare. However, the opinions
expressed herein do not necessarily reflect the
position or policy of that Agency, and no official
endorsement should be inferred.

FOREWORD

Roger Baty's research was based on the recognition that it is dysfunctional to think of American culture as a homogeneous set of values or of behaviors; the popular image of America as a "pot" within which differences are melted into a single blended stew is not congruent with social reality. The prime instrument of acculturation in the past has been the American public school, but it is now obvious that we can no longer accept without question this traditional function of our educational system. Cultural diversity both in the classroom and in the society has been ignored to the detriment of individual students and national unity.

An acceptance of the classroom as a place for supporting cultural diversity creates a stress for both teacher and student. Traditionally, under an acculturation philosophy, it was the responsibility of the child from the different culture to adjust to the teacher, the curriculum, and the norms of the school. The acceptance of cultural diversity means that the teacher must also accommodate himself to the culture of the child from a minority background.

This description of that process in a particular school reveals how difficult this accommodation is. Learning to recognize the cues that indicate feelings and attitudes of students from an ethnic community toward the teacher and her behavior in the classroom requires special experience, perhaps direct interpersonal confrontation. In this study, with its action component, Baty took time to understand the complexities of this process and the importance of involving the adult community and the school in the effort to bring about better communication between the teacher and her students. His account of the teachers' experiences in responding to the community's message and his report of the resulting changes in the teaching staff constitute a useful addition to the growing literature on educational and political issues involved in cultural diversity within this country.

Robert D. Hess

ACKNOWLEDGMENTS

If there be kudos for this study, let it be shared. Most important, let it be shared by my wife, whose persistent optimism kept me from weariness, also by my colleagues and mentors of three years at SIDEC, whose contributions were not only through empathy, but also through piquant criticism.

I would like to record here my thanks to Kathleen and Bernard J. Fisken, who contributed inspiration and helped me gain entree in the field. The superintendent of the Whisman School District, Ross Carter, and the Whisman School Board went out of their way on numerous occasions to provide me with the solid support needed for the project. Through their help and that of the superintendents of the Mountain View and Sunnyvale Elementary School Districts, I was able to recruit teachers for the training program. Without the interested teachers, of course, there would have been no study. This work is dedicated to those classroom teachers who consistently demonstrated their willingness to work far beyond the call of duty in order to become better educators.

The speakers whose presentations formed the core of the training program are to be thanked. Men are hard to find who have the qualities of Albert Piñon, Hector Abeytia, L. M. Lopez, Professor Mac Martinez, John Plakos, Leonard Olguin, David Downing, Walter J. Symons, Richard Mesa, Ernest J. Paramo, Charles J. Bustamante, and Antonio del Buono.

Special thanks are due Yervant Andelian, Arthur Lopez, Robert Nava, and Richard Rios for their contributions as discussion leaders.

Invaluable insights, advice, and encouragement were rendered at numerous critical steps along the way by Arthur P. Coladarci, Robert D. Hess, and George D. Spindler. I am particularly grateful to Dr. Hess, who inspired self-confidence, but not overconfidence.

CONTENTS

Appendix	Page

LIST OF TABLES

TABLES IN THE APPENDIXES

Appendix Table		Page

LIST OF FIGURES

FIGURES IN THE APPENDIX

Reeducating Teachers for Cultural Awareness

CHAPTER 1

INTRODUCTION

NATURE OF THE STUDY

This is an action-research study designed to determine the effect of exposure to cultural, social, and economic diversity on selected attitudes of elementary school teachers. The research developed two thrusts. One was to investigate the effects of exposure to the usual classroom situation on teacher tolerance and teacher optimism. The other was to investigate the effects of exposure to an in-service training program, in addition to the usual classroom situation.

The study is interdisciplinary in scope in that the generation of hypotheses, the selection of an appropriate setting, and the techniques for managing the study in the field are derived from three domains of intellectual inquiry: compensatory education, anthropology, and planned change. The relevant area of compensatory education is labeled "teachers of the disadvantaged," or "teachers of the culturally different." The subset of anthropology that is relevant to the inquiry is the phenomenon of acculturation. Guidelines for the implementation of the study in the field are drawn from the theory and practice of introducing planned change at the community level.

The dependent variables--optimism about pupil potential to achieve and tolerance of minority self-assertiveness--were selected for their relevance to current inquiry in the broad area of preparing teachers to work more effectively with urban and suburban children.

ORIENTATION OF THE RESEARCHER

Action-research is fraught with difficulties. Action-research involving field experiments is particularly difficult since there are so many variables which may affect the course of the experiment. The researcher usually attempts to control for some variables by being quiet about what he is doing, hoping that by keeping information from his subjects, he will not bias the experiment in the direction predicted by his theory. Other variables that are not controlled for are assumed to be at work in random fashion, influencing subjects in the treatment and nontreatment groups in similar ways, thus making it reasonable to assume that final differences are outcomes of the treatment rather than the effects of other factors.

One of the variables that cannot be held constant in an experiment such as the one carried out in this study is the personality of the researcher himself. It is not possible for the researcher to be involved in equal degrees with the treatment and nontreatment groups. Nevertheless, it is possible and, indeed, necessary that the researcher state the point of view which underlies and may possibly influence the results of his research. An open description of such assumptions is as close as the social scientist can come to objectivity.

Holding with this view, it is believed that the causation of social problems such as poverty and ignorance resides in the affluent and well-educated sectors of the society as well as in the relatively impoverished and poorly educated sectors. In the field of compensatory education, for example, problems of the "disadvantaged" learner are not caused entirely by the conditions of a child's upbringing that limit the extent of his identification with the middle-class curriculum and his participation in the school programs. The problems of the "disadvantaged learner" are also caused by the inability of the teacher to make the learning experience relevant to the child's background. Teachers often fail to find out how a child's readiness for learning might be approached. Consequently, the lessons lack relevance and meaning. The child who does not understand the meaning of the lesson fails to profit from it and falls farther and farther behind, due to the teacher's inadequacies as well as his own.

Contributing to the development of what might be termed a "minority" point of view were the experiences gained through two years of residence and community-based experience in East Palo Alto, California, an area near the site chosen for the research study. Through encounter and association with minority people as neighbors and as fellow members of community-work committees, insight was gained of the points of view of the Black community and the Mexican-American community. One of the outcomes was an awareness of the extent to which social, cultural, and economic cleavages influence the behavior patterns in our society.

This awareness of cleavages in our society may be thought of as part of the _zeitgeist_, the spirit of the times, which is marked by a heightened awareness of the complex etiology of social problems. Political leaders as well as scholars have begun to devote more attention to these matters. The Report of the National Advisory Commission on Civil Disorders (1968) (the Kerner Commission Report) illustrates the attention being given by political leaders. Illustrative of the increasing concern of scholars is the following excerpt from an article by Robert D. Hess (1968: 529):

> In the past, the schools have served an acculturating, melting-pot function, providing common allegiance and values to bring together in a single country immigrant groups from different ethnic and national backgrounds. It now seems, however, that the ethnic and cultural differences within the nation cannot be easily blended into unity. Divergences and inequities which have been ignored, particularly with respect to Negroes in the society, are dramatically apparent. It is evident to many citizens that the picture of unity, equality, and freedom that is so often presented is distorted, oversimplified, and, to a degree, false. Indeed, political socialization in the schools may have created an attitude of complacency, a willingness to accept the image of unity and freedom--as well as the actions of the government--and, in so doing, it may have contributed to the feelings of disillusionment and the consequent climate of protest. It is by no means assured that the schools can now deal with the issues of political socialization that these new conditions present or that adequate changes can be effected which would provide more relevant teaching of political attitudes, values, and behaviors.

As this statement indicates, these are times when old assumptions are being challenged. Many people are now engaged in the search for viable alternative assumptions and approaches to the task of preparing the young for adult roles. One approach, urged by Hess, is that of recognizing the situation as it exists and training children in the schools to cope with reality and not exclusively with ideals--to involve in the training emotion and action in addition to cognition. The point to be made is that new approaches must be discovered if the educational system is to play a part in relieving some of the internal problems facing American Society.

Many efforts during the late 1960's have been focused on improving the educational opportunities of "disadvantaged" children. The assumption has been that the source of the difficulty lies in the cognitive deficit which disadvantaged children bring with them to the classroom. This deficit makes cumulative retardation and the ensuing gap between advantaged and disadvantaged inevitable. Much less attention has been given to the need for reeducation of adults in the educational system, especially teachers and administrators. Yet, without changes in attitude and behavior of those who are responsible for the education of the young, it is difficult to see how any lasting changes can be brought about. The action-research program described here represents an attempt at finding ways of inducing desired changes. In keeping with the point of view described above, the book takes a fresh look at the public educational institutions, this time not focusing on the usual objects of research, the "culturally disadvantaged" students, but rather on their "culturally disadvantaged" teachers.

CHAPTER 2

FORMULATING THE RESEARCH DESIGN

THE PROBLEM AREA: TEACHERS OF THE DISADVANTAGED

Numerous studies of the disadvantaged child have been undertaken in recent years (Deutsch 1964; Gray and Klaus 1963; Goldstein 1967; Passow 1963; Stodolsky and Lesser 1968). One of the conclusions drawn from such studies is that the disadvantaged child is handicapped by a curriculum that is irrelevant to his needs and requirements (Bloom, Davis, and Hess 1965: 21). It has also been found that minority and/or poor children consistently perform less satisfactorily on tasks designed to measure intellectual performance than do children from majority, middle-class groups (Stodolsky and Lesser 1968). Another factor contributing to the difficulties of the disadvantaged learner is a critical shortage of teachers who understand the children well enough to communicate effectively with them (McCloskey 1967; Groff 1967; Fuchs 1968).*

Although there is a critical shortage of teachers who understand minority and/or poor children, there

---

*The bulk of work done in the field of compensatory education has centered on the disadvantaged child. Relatively little study has been made of the teacher of the disadvantaged. For example, in a reference document for the Research Conference on Education and Cultural Deprivation held at the University of Chicago in 1964, 104 of the works reviewed dealt primarily with the child, whereas only 4 works dealt with the teacher (Bloom, Davis, and Hess 1965: 67ff).

have been relatively few studies of attempts to increase the supply of effective teachers. There are descriptive studies which help account for the shortage of effective teachers (Haubrich 1963). There have also been studies listing the attributes that teachers of the disadvantaged should possess (Goldberg 1967: 472; Trubowitz 1968). Reports have been published describing training programs for teachers in urban ghettos (Haubrich 1963; Ornstein 1967). There are, however, few studies of attempts to increase the supply of effective teachers by reeducating those teachers already on the job and improving their attitudes toward minority and/or poor people. There is a need for such studies, which would yield comparative data on changes in teacher attitudes with and without supplemental training programs.

THE THEORETICAL CONTEXT

The theoretical context of the research is the acculturation process, described by Alan Beals (1967: 220) as "the most important of the processes involved in cultural change." Acculturation has also been defined as "culture change that is initiated by the conjunction of two or more autonomous cultural systems" (Broom *et al*. 1967: 256, 257). Those same authors further state that

> cultural changes induced by contacts between ethnic enclaves and their encompassing societies would be definable as acculturative, whereas those resulting from the interactions of factions, classes, occupational groups, or other specialized categories within a single society would not be so considered.

In order to justify relating this study to the process of acculturation, it is argued that the analysis is one of contacts between ethnic enclaves and their encompassing society. It is further argued that since, owing to patterns of habitation, ethnic subcultures have developed within the larger culture, it is reasonable to treat them as subsets of the larger society, distinct from it in important ways (Heller 1966). Thus, the ghetto, whether or not characteristic of the living patterns of poor Whites, Negroes, or Mexican-Americans, can be analyzed as a cultural subset within a larger society modally described as European in ancestry and middle-class in socio-economic status. Regarded from this point of view, the school becomes one of the most important contact points between the larger society and its subsets. In the schools, the values, beliefs, history, and skills of the larger society are "offered" the young people of the subgroup or minority group by the teachers acting as the agents of the "encompassing society." The school is a primary "contact situation" where acculturative influences are brought to bear not only on the children but on the teachers as well.

Use of the term "acculturation" is somewhat different in this study from its use by Leonard Broom and his colleagues. While they considered the unit of analysis to be "any given culture as it is carried by its particular society" (Broom *et al*. 1967: 258), it is considered here to be the elementary school teacher. In so doing, the approach more closely resembles that taken by G. D. Spindler (1963: 144), who used "acculturation" to refer to the "changes brought about in the culture of groups or individuals as adaptation to a culture different from their own takes place."

The acculturation process has been used to explain difficulties encountered by disadvantaged students in the schools. Hilda Taba (1966: 230), for example, presented the view that the school is an alien, unfamiliar culture to those from "culturally deviant backgrounds." According to Taba, such children face "acculturation shock," which can seriously hamper their ability to cope with school work.

A similar analysis could be made of the teacher who confronts culturally different children for the first time, especially when cultural difference is combined with low socio-economic level.* Allison Davis (1964) expressly described teacher difficulties in terms of emotional trauma equivalent to culture shock. Other writers have described the difficulties of incoming teachers without relating the description to acculturation. The following quotation from Vernon Haubrich (1963: 246) illustrates this point:

---

*Beals pointed out that very little attention has been given in acculturation studies to the changes brought about in the dominant groups as a result of culture contact. The present design considers teachers the contact agents for the dominant culture, and the research question asks what effect exposure to the subordinate group has on the contact agents. In pursuing

> The incoming teacher probably rejects the situation because of an inability to comprehend, understand, and cope with the multiple problems of language development, varying social norms, habits not accepted by the teacher, behavior which is often not success-oriented, lack of student "cooperation," and achievement levels well below expectancies of teachers.

Haubrich described an acculturative reaction without calling it that. Other writers have mentioned the fact that teachers prefer to avoid urban ghetto schools (Sexton 1961). Such an observation acquires more meaning when interpreted as one of the alternative behavior patterns open to an individual confronted with an alien culture (Spindler 1963).

Although it is apparent from the literature that contact with disadvantaged children may have a negative effect on teachers' attitudes, there have been neither attempts to measure this effect nor reported attempts to measure the extent to which negative effects can be offset by appropriate training programs. This research attempts both tasks--to measure the effects, on teacher attitudes, of exposure to disadvantaged children in the classroom (the *status quo*), and to compare this with the effect of supplemental inservice training.

THE RESEARCH DESIGN

The research was conducted as a field experiment using a pretest-posttest control group design with replication. A summer of preliminary field work was required to set the stage for the experiment. Teachers who volunteered to participate were matched on several background variables and randomly allocated to a treatment group and a comparison group. (See Appendix A.) Both groups received the pretest before being informed of their group membership. The treatment group took the training program in the autumn quarter. Both groups were given the posttest. The control group

---

this approach, the recommendation of Richard Thurwald is also followed. Thurwald, as early as 1935, emphasized the need to "understand not only the agents of acculturation and their motivations, but the changes which take place in the agents as a result of the contact situation" (Beals 1953: 635).

received the training program in the winter quarter and again received the posttest. Teacher interviews were held with participants from both training programs. In diagrammatic form, the design appears in Figure 1.

FIGURE 1

Diagram of Research Design

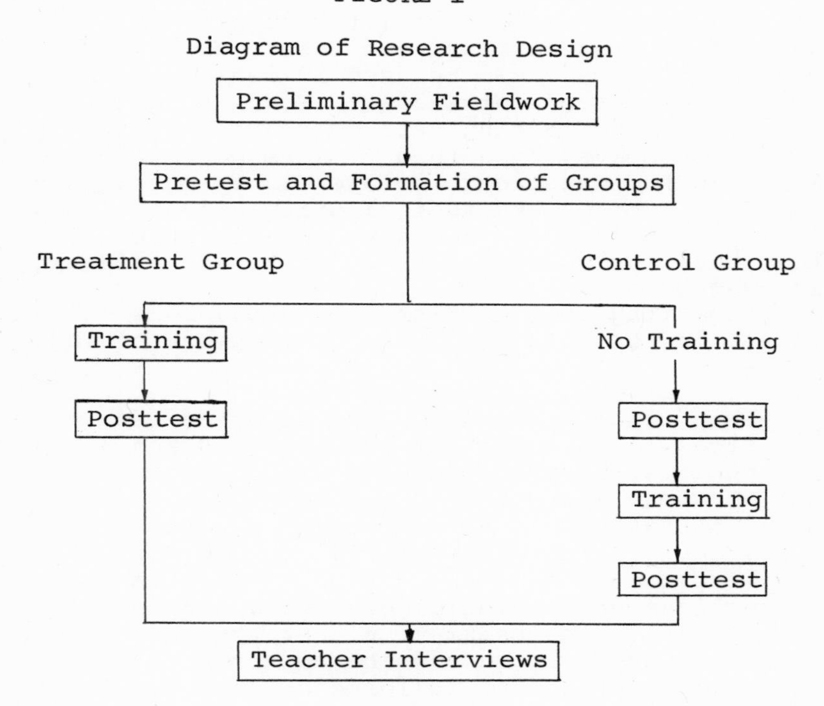

The research design permits consideration of the following questions:

1. Were there significant differences in teacher attitudes to begin with, due to differences in prior experience and background?

2. Were there significant measurable changes in teacher attitudes as a result of exposure to the classroom situation without a training program?

3. Were there significant measurable changes in teacher attitudes as a result of exposure to the classroom situation and a training program?

4. Did training make a difference?

5. Could the results of the training program be replicated?

6. Were there other results of the training program which had practical significance, but which were not detected by the instruments used to measure change?

THE INSTRUMENT FOR DATA COLLECTION

Given the problem area, teachers of the disadvantaged, it was necessary to locate or develop an instrument which could be used in measuring changes in relevant teacher attitudes. The instrument finally selected for collecting data on teacher attitudes was an opinion survey by Harold A. Jonsson (1968). Contained in the questionnaire are eighty-one items that probe two complex attitudinal orientations: "optimistic orientation toward achievement potential" and "tolerance for self-assertiveness by educationally disadvantaged."

Regarding the optimism dimension, Jonsson (1968) states, in his account of the development of the instrument:

> This crucial-variable dimension has been stressed in several recent studies and publications dealing with the education of the disadvantaged. For example, the constant burden of the Haryou Report [_Youth in the Ghetto_, 1964] is that the single most damaging factor in limiting achievement potential of disadvantaged pupils is the assumption that the children _cannot learn_ and the acceptance of their substandard performance as inevitable (p. 229 and passim). Those successes achieved in experimental programs are viewed as resulting from "an application of the conviction that lower-class children can learn" (p. 242) and the overwhelming conclusion of the report is that "effective remedies will come only from a firm belief and insistence that the pupils _can_ perform. . . ." (p. 244). A similar emphasis is made by Bowers, Masia, and Medley (1966, 28). In answering the question, "What specific teacher behaviors and attitudes are appropriate to the educational characteristics and needs of children handicapped by social and economic disadvantage?", these

> authors place optimistic orientation at the top of their list: "Probably the overriding demand of teachers of disadvantaged children is for an attitudinal commitment to hope and expectation that these children can learn and that the teacher can create the necessary conditions to permit effective learning."
>
> The same point is made by such diverse spokesmen as Francis Keppel (1966), Floyd McKissick (1966) and Kenneth Clark (1965). It is increasingly recognized that empathy, acceptance, and teacher-pupil rapport cannot alone activate the achievement potential of the disadvantaged, but must be accompanied by a powerful and well-directed optimism and expectation with regard to this potential.

Jonsson formulated the tolerance scale "to ascertain attitudes toward rising Black militancy and the relationship between such attitudes and optimistic orientation." He left the relationship to be determined empirically.

In the conclusion of his report of the scale development Jonsson (1968: D-6) states: "The validity and reliability data are sufficiently encouraging to warrant the further refinement and use of these scales. The need for measures in these areas is supported by virtually all of the recent literature in the field of the educationally disadvantaged."

Sources of data besides the questionnaire included participation in the course, feedback from discussion leaders, class evaluation forms, tapes of discussion sessions, observation of classrooms and informal discussion with teachers outside of class-time.

CHAPTER 3

IMPLEMENTING THE RESEARCH DESIGN

FIELDWORK LEADING TO THE TRAINING PROGRAM

Theoretical Guidelines

The task of locating a suitable research site, and building the infrastructure for the training program required several months. The theoretical guidelines followed were those of Lippitt, *et al*. (1958). These authors regard the change process as a series of phases. Initially, there is recognition of a problem in a given target area. Following such recognition is development of a working relationship between a change agent (in this case, the researcher) and the client system (in this case, three participating school districts). During this phase, the time perspectives are clarified and the various subparts of school and community to be involved are asked to agree on the basic outline of the plan to be followed. In the third phase, the problem or salient problems of the client system are clarified. Goals are then established, and alternative routes for attaining these goals are examined. The intentions are then transformed into action. Once intentions have been transformed into actual change efforts, the attempt is made to ensure that the changes brought about are stabilized. The common hazard is for the system to revert to its old pattern once the change effort ceases.

The phases of introducing change which Lippitt, Watson, and Westley outlined were consciously adhered to in developing the foundation for the course. It was thought that omitting a phase would quite likely create additional problems later on. Since a necessary condition for the entire effort was the fostering and maintaining trust between the researcher and the leaders of the school and minority community, it was necessary to proceed slowly, to allow time for the initiative to come from the community and the school, rather than exclusively from the researcher.

Location of a Research Site

Several communities in the southern Bay region, containing significant minority populations, were suggested as possible sites. A series of exploratory interviews with teachers combined with a study of census data and travels through the region helped narrow the possibilities to five. These were arranged according to a set of priorities that included the type of predominant minority group, the general socio-economic level of the community, and the ease of access.

As the search for a suitable location progressed, it became increasingly obvious that there was intense resistance in the Black community to being "researched." Therefore, a site was sought where the school officials and minority community leaders would accept the research team and admittance to the community would be for the overt purpose of undertaking research. At the same time, activity with the Black community could continue with no risk of that activity being construed as a front for covert research.*

The community finally chosen was similar in many respects to the community in which we resided. While the predominant minority group in the research setting was Mexican-American rather than Black, the former group, as well as the latter was becoming increasingly

---

*It should be remembered that the decisions regarding the location of the research were being made at a time of intense social trouble (spring and summer, 1968). The intensity of the problems of social development within this country was being made painfully obvious, by King's assassination, followed by Kennedy's; by student unrest over Vietnam; by publication of the Report of the National Advisory Commission on Civil Disorders. The decision to conduct our research outside our place of residence in an overt way was a source of considerable peace of mind and a means of reducing the personal hazards associated with out community activities, both at our place of residence and at the research site.

self-conscious and self-assertive, demanding better housing, jobs, and education. In both groups there was intense distrust of the white power structure. However, one difference between the two communities was the visibility of the predominant minority group. In the research setting, the minority population was scattered in small enclaves over a relatively large area, rather than concentrated geographically. There was only one census tract in the research area, for example, in which the concentration of Mexican-Americans was as high as 19 percent. The average for the school districts involved was about 8 percent. The proportion of Mexican-Americans of school age, however, was not reflected by the general census tract data. The proportion of Mexican-American children in the school districts that became involved in the project was approximately twice as high as the census tract figures suggested for the general population.

First official contact with the area was with Ross Carter, Superintendent of the Whisman School District. He strongly supported the nature of the research interest and explained the general type of problems faced by his and neighboring school districts. Pressure was being brought to bear on the schools by the Mexican-Americans. They wanted the schools to raise the self-esteem of their children. They wanted the second language and other abilities of the students to be recognized. They wanted teachers who showed racial bias to undergo sensitivity training. Officials had received threats of Molotov cocktails.

To improve the existing situation, Superintendent Carter was encouraging a program of general curriculum revision from kindergarten through junior college. He was also keenly interested in developing a model program that would assist other districts being pressured to respond to the needs of the minority communities. In relation to this, the task which seemed to be most within the capabilities of the researchers would be that of setting up an in-service training program for teachers of Mexican-American children. It was agreed to wait for a few days before making any definite commitment.

Investigation of the Feasibility of Involvement

During those few days, follow-up conversations were held with other staff members in order to get more of a picture of the history of the district's relationship with the Mexican-American minority. Knowledge was sought as to whether sufficient groundwork had been developed to make it reasonable to assume that a "felt need" for in-service training existed in the teachers and administrators in the district.

Interviews, conversations, meetings, and a study of reports suggested the hypothesis that there were a number of teachers with little understanding of the problems of the Mexican-American community. Meetings with Mexican-American educators the previous year had been held, but these meetings had involved primarily administrators. One formal meeting between teachers and Mexican-American parents had been held a few weeks earlier to begin dialogue between the two groups. Although the discussants were very defensive at first--the educators saying it was up to the parents and the parents saying it was up to the schools--the meeting ended with general agreement that something should be done.

The Whisman School District was already pioneering in the area of curriculum change, particularly at the preschool level. Volunteer reading programs aimed at building up children's self-esteem had been operating for three years. Speech therapists who were also language development specialists were used in these.

A preschool program similar to Head Start, underway for two years, had involved some sixty children. For three years there had been a program for children of working mothers, which involved some 110 youngsters. It was apparent, however, that the focus of past efforts had been on the development of programs that would "enrich" the background of the children. The time seemed appropriate for a deliberate effort to increase the cultural sensitivities of the teachers to help them become more aware of the cultural heritage the children bring with them to class.

In these conversations encouragement was found for the idea of a course that would expose the teachers to the cultural heritage and historical background of Mexican-Americans. Such a course could also give the teachers some motivational tips. What, for example, could be done to encourage bilingualism at each grade level? How could family traditions be reinforced? It was suggested by Jessie Kobayashi, Director of Curriculum for the Whisman District, that a course should get across some basic understandings, such as the fact that a different diet may be nutritionally acceptable, or that a teacher must become acquainted with the home situation in order to understand child and adult behavior. It was recognized that such an effort would contribute to the long-term goal of more and healthier dialogue between the minority community and the school system, which would be beneficial for all concerned.

There was substantial support at the top administrative levels for the idea of an in-service training program. The next step was to determine the extent to which such a program would be satisfactory to the Mexican-American leaders and other people in the community outside the school system. It was thought essential that community leaders find the course responding to needs they expressed and not interpret it as a stalling tactic on the part of the district.

For some weeks, pressure on the school system had been mounting from two sources: one, a group of Mexican-American parents organized through the work of the local Office of Economic Opportunity, directed by Richard Cabrera; and the other, a group of Anglo (white) parents who believed their children were suffering from lack of contact with the Mexican-American community. Toward the latter part of the 1968 school year, the group of concerned Mexican-American parents presented the following memo to the district educators:

> During the past several weeks a group of Mexican-American parents has met both with local educators and by themselves.
>
> As a group we are concerned that the educational level of our children remains very low. Our children's drop-out rate in high school is disastrous.
>
> We are the largest single minority in the Southwest. Now over 5 million strong we are less educated than the Negro. As a result we make less money. We have larger families and poorer homes. We are determined not to leave this heritage to our children.
>
> We therefore respectfully make the following suggestions:
>
> 1. That positive emphasis on the culture and history of the Mexican-American be stressed in all classes and at all levels. This can be accomplished not only by guest speakers, but also by teachers' making frequent references to the Mexican-American heritage.
>
> 2. That maximum use be made of available professional resources such as Stanford, Cal. [University of California at Berkely], Far West Laboratories, U.C.L.A. Study Project, etc.

3. That sociograms measuring racial bias be prepared to determine the Mexican-American student's attitude toward his teachers. Non-Mexican-American students should be used as the control group.

4. That those educators whom the students feel are racially biased undergo sensitivity training.

5. That those teachers whom the students feel are not racially biased find ways and means to demonstrate their non-bias.

6. That upper grade students doing poorly in a particular subject teach that same subject to lower grade students (4-5 years behind them).

7. That teachers at every level urge Mexican-American children to speak and practice Spanish and that teachers use Mexican-American students to help their classmates learn the correct pronunciation of Spanish.

8. That special Spanish courses for college credit be developed at the high school level for Mexican-American children. And that these courses be publicized both within the school systems and the community at large.

9. That the flexible schedule currently in existence at Mountain View High School be more structured for those doing poorly, particularly in the areas in which they lag.

10. That something other than expulsion be found as means of punishing students.

11. That in extreme cases when expulsion is deemed necessary, the staff of Area Service Center Nine be advised of each and every expulsion.

12. That teachers and administrators continue to meet with this group of concerned parents and the Service Center staff.

13. That many more Mexican-American counselors, teachers and teacher aids be hired by the Schools.

The above recommendations are made with the sincere hope that parents and teachers can work together to improve the educational level of our children.

> We are fully aware that the home, where preliminary socialization takes place, has a major responsibility for the education and preparation of children. We are also aware that playmates and preliminary peer groups contribute greatly to who and what the student is.
>
> We must nevertheless insist that the educator is trained to educate. He has devoted his life to helping children obtain knowledge. He gets paid to teach; and yet for one reason or another he is not teaching our children.
>
> We simply cannot allow our children to go uneducated. The price is far too high and the time indeed too late!
>
> Ya basta!!! We have had enough!!!

About a month later, some Anglo parents stated their point of view in a letter to the High School Superintendent:

> As you know, we feel that racism is an ingrained ingredient in our society due in large part to institutional negligence and omission. We are certain that our schools can and must root out many facets of minority problems. Our children need preparation for their kind of world. They must be able to honestly scrutinize the lurid inequities which exist in our country, and others, historically as well as currently. They must be able to honor the validity and strengths of varied cultures. And the schools must educate toward these goals.
>
> We hope that you and the School Board will consider and take action upon:
>
> 1. Workshops for all teachers with lecturers from minority groups "to tell it like it really is."
> 2. Reevaluation and broadening of social studies and literature curricula, based upon further study workshops.
> 3. Active recruiting and hiring of members of minority groups in classified as well as credentialed positions. We would desire a broad base rather than tokenism.
> 4. Ways to fulfill the educational aspirations of student members of minority

> groups, and to assure their consideration as vital participants in the school community. . . .

The parents urged that their letter and the results of an earlier meeting with school officials be placed on the agenda of the next meeting of the school board.

The contents of the letter revealed a growing realization on the part of some of the majority group for the need to become more informed. It also reinforced the approach which had been planned for the training program, namely, to invite lecturers from the relevant minority group to present their views to the teachers.

Decision to Commit Further Resources

The two communications quoted above were evidence of a growing concern in the community at large that the schools had neglected certain of their responsibilities. The letters indicated that a need for change was felt at the local level by both Anglos and Mexican-Americans. The constructive tone of the letters suggested there was still time to respond in the direction outlined in the communications: namely, the preparation of a training program proposal.

Development of the Training Program Proposal

Given apparent community support, the next step was to develop contacts outside the target area and to survey current projects being undertaken elsewhere. The intention was to become as familiar as possible with what was going on in the field, in order to prepare a proposal that was in keeping with emerging best practices.

In the course of the conversations with professionals and staff members of field projects, successful teaching practices were sought by asking the question, What works? Efforts were also made to identify techniques, of bringing about changes in teachers, that might be employed in the training program.*

---

*An interview with Jack Forbes of the Far West Laboratory for Educational Research and Development illustrates the point. Forbes stressed the need for programs with a greater impact on the teacher than

In conjunction with field visits, teacher supervisors and teachers themselves were interviewed to get a better picture of the nature of the teachers' difficulty with Mexican-American children. Attempts were also made to find illustrations of cultural understandings that might have a practical significance or "pay-off" for the teacher and students in the classroom.

One researcher interviewed thought that the Anglo teachers were unable to relate to the Mexican-American children. "They use the wrong approach," he maintained. "They encourage independence and competitiveness, which is fine for the Anglo, middle-class youngster, but they neglect to encourage cooperativeness and fail to provide the warmth the Mexican-American child needs." This failure to provide for the needs of the Mexican-American child was unfortunate because of the importance of the teacher's role. "The home is important, but the teacher really has the greatest responsibility. The principal can also encourage, but in the final analysis, it is the teacher who interacts more with the children." Comments such as these helped clarify the problem.

Further Definition of the Problem

Teachers, by nature of their background and training, lack knowledge about students whose backgrounds are different from their own. In the classroom, this results in what might be best termed "cultural blindness." Many teachers would agree with the teacher who told the researcher: "I apply my same standards to Mexican-American children that I apply to all children. I love them, have fun with them, respect them as individuals, expect them to respect me, and discipline them as I do Anglo children." In short, the teacher is saying she treats them "all the same." What in fact takes place is the handing out of a single treatment to children

---

was typical. He thought the ideal method would be to bring the teachers together for an entire month of intensive training prior to the opening of school. Such an approach would probably be potent enough to have a decisive impact on teacher attitudes. (We were unable to follow up on Forbes' suggestion, but a future proposal could incorporate the idea of an intensive preschool training program, something like a VISTA or Peace Corps training program.)

who have different backgrounds and who are, as a result, interpreting what the teacher says in different ways. Looking at the problem the other way, if a teacher assumes she treats all children the same but fails to differentiate their responses on the basis of their cultural background, she is in fact failing to communicate with the children who do not use her own language, "silent" as well as "spoken."

An excellent illustration of the point involves the position of the head and eyes of the child when being disciplined by the adult. Anglo teachers in the early grades almost uniformly demand eye contact when disciplining a child. A common thing to do is hold the child by the shoulder or under the chin and say, "Now you look at me!" Very often the teacher does not realize that in many families of Latin background, a child being chastized is required to look at the floor as a sign of respect or else receive a cascaron (knuckle) on the forehead. The teacher who is unaware of the training the child has received at home will often interpret the Mexican child's downward gaze as a sign of stubbornness or uncooperativeness rather than as a sign of respect. The consequences on interpersonal relations between teacher and student are damaging and totally unnecessary--but this is what is likely to happen when the teacher treats them "all the same." For a lucid description of the problem, see Spindler (1959).

Language presented some of the greatest difficulties. One field worker suggested that the child does not pick up the appropriate cues from the teacher's speech. It was plausible to reason that the child therefore fails to respond in a way the teacher recognizes as appropriate. The teacher, not knowing how to cope with the situation, communicates her frustration to the child. The child does not understand the verbal cues the teacher gives, but does interpret the facial expression, gesture, and other signs of frustration and dismay as indications of the child's failure. The result may well be self-fulfilling.*

---

*Not all problems were seen to stem from teacher inadequacies or ignorance. Some of those interviewed felt the teacher was a victim of circumstances. "Change the nature of the evaluation of teachers," they said, "and you will change teachers. If the achievement scores of the students are considered important, teachers will stress the subjects that

Positive Teacher Style

Some teachers' discovery of cultural phenomena helped them manage their classrooms. One teacher, for example, described how her approach to a Mexican-American child who was causing behavior problems in the classroom was modified when she learned that the male figure has the authority in the Mexican home. Rather than try to assert her own authority, she relied on the authority of the father to improve the child's behavior.

One characteristic of the Mexican-American children often mentioned was their lack of self-esteem. Consequently, a question asked practitioners was, "How do you raise the self-esteem of the youngsters?" One teacher did not give a verbal answer but invited the viewing of her class of preschool Mexican-American children who were participants in a Head Start program. The following description is taken from that day's field notes:

> At 9 A.M., Miss C. seated herself on a small chair in front of a flannel board in one corner of the room. In front of her feet was a large oval rug. As the children came into the room they were greeted by the teacher and then took their places on the rug. In greeting the students, the teacher spoke to each one by name using the Spanish pronunciation of their name. She inquired of some about their elder brothers and sisters. Others she asked to tell her what they had brought to show the class that day.
>
> When they were all seated, she asked what they had brought to show the class. Each of those who had brought something took his turn standing by the teacher and showing what he had brought. The teacher put her arm around each one as he spoke and prompted him with short questions.
>
> Usually the children appeared quite bashful and shy, preferring to talk to her rather than to the class. One heavy-set boy had no trouble telling the group

---

appear on the achievement tests. If English scores are carefully looked at, English will be stressed." Teacher evaluation was seen to be a major source of the present difficulties.

of thirteen about the slingshot he had recently acquired.

Occasionally, when other students started to tell the story for the one who was standing in front, the teacher would remind them gently that each person should tell his own story. She would say, for example, "Let Jesus tell the story. He has a mouth too."

When each one was finished telling about what he had brought, the youngster then placed the item over on a table near the door. Items included a cookie, some color crayons, a scrap book with some of the pictures torn out, and, of course, the slingshot.

After showing their possessions to the class, they all stood up and skipped twice around the room after the teacher, singing a little song. Once back to the rug, they started talking about pets--dogs, cats, and kittens. Several students told about the dogs they had or wanted to have. All the children were encouraged to say something.

At the end of the period, the class divided into small groups to work with older high school students and I took advantage of the opportunity to discuss what I had observed with the teacher. I mentioned how impressed I was by the knowledge which she had of the families of the children. She said that this was because she had grown up in the neighborhood and knew all the families. When I asked further about the approach she used, she found it difficult to describe what her methods were or why she was a successful teacher. She said she treated them as any children, not as though they were different or as though she felt sorry for them. She wanted to show them the attention and love which any child wants. "I may be too close to the situation," she said, "to really be able to say what I am doing."

Although the teacher herself was unable to say just why she had such good rapport with her students, several things suggested an effective style. She was not aggressive, but warm. She did not rush to the children to greet them, but she personally received them as they came to her with their morning greeting. Her clothes were probably like the clothes the children were used to seeing adults wear--not dressy, but neat and soft rather than starchy. She wore no jewelry and did not otherwise set herself apart from the children's own socio-economic background. She did not have her hair "done up." Miss C. knew the families the children were from. She knew their older brothers and sisters, and in turn was no doubt known by them. She lived in the neighborhood and did not have the problems of "relating" that an outsider would have. The habits of the children were habits with which she was familiar. Nor did she have trouble accepting them. She mentioned her Italian ancestry as perhaps playing a part in fostering understanding. She also spoke Spanish, although no Spanish, save for the pronunciation of the children's names, was used in class.

It was apparent that the variable of "culture" was not a critical one in this instance, because the differences between the children and their teacher had been reduced to the point where they were no longer a source of misunderstanding. Culture was important in this instance, not because it was a variable consciously worked with, but because the features that comprise "culture" were so well understood, that there was, in effect, no cultural barrier separating teacher from students.

Submission of the Proposal

After several weeks of intensive searching, visiting, interviewing and listening, the needs of the community and the level the teachers had reached in their understanding of the Mexican-American people became clear. By pulling together the various suggestions that were made and adding these to some useful components of Peace Corps training programs, a proposed training program was drawn up and approved by the school districts.

Development of the Training Program

Attention was next concentrated on the multifaceted task of making the training program operational. One of the first critical decisions concerned the structure of the program. This had been discussed tentatively with educational leaders earlier in the summer but the time had come for making decisions.

It was decided to combine formal lectures with discussion groups. The lecturers would be for the most part, Mexican-Americans, whose qualifications would lie in their experiences, personal insights, and ability to communicate to the teachers.* Each presentation of information would be followed by a discussion group. The key to participating in the discussion groups would be involvement. The discussion leaders would try to give the teachers the opportunity to express their own views and look for ways of making what they were learning relevant to their classroom situations. Classroom materials would be given the teachers so that they would be provided with new inputs of information which, when used in the classroom, would result in an experience that would probably challenge some of the ideas held earlier, while confirming others.

The search for Mexican-Americans who could interpret the culture to the teachers was pursued inside and outside the district. Ongoing projects in other locations were visited to become acquainted with the reputations of leaders from the Mexican-American community. Many of these leaders were later approached and invited to participate as lecturers. Not all of those invited were able to serve. Vacations or trips to other parts of the country prohibited some from speaking. Financial considerations prevented others. One of those who attached a higher price to his services than was offered said that he was through being exploited. Mexican Culture was his specialty, he said, and he would not consider participating for anything less than a professional fee of $150 for an evening's presentation. He thought it was time the school districts began to realize that they could not begin to tackle the problems of the minorities without spending some money on the task. "Schools should no longer expect volunteers to do their work for them," he stated.

---

*The model for this method of identifying strategically placed community leaders is a modification of the Hunter "reputational technique." We asked selected persons at the center of activity in this field to nominate the Mexican-American leaders who could do the best job of interpreting Mexican-American culture to teachers. From this list were finally selected those who were invited to participate in the program as lecturers. Source of the description of the Hunter technique is Kimbrough (1964: 29).

Many days were spent visiting projects, attending community programs and activities, and following up leads with letters and personal visits. Gradually the number of those who had agreed to lecture was increased.

Midway through the summer, invaluable assistance was received from a gentleman highly placed in the administration of migrant education projects in the county, Ernest Paramo. He took a personal interest in the project. It was through his assistance that many of the lecturers were finally engaged in the program. Many of those who lectured did so as a personal favor to Paramo.

In addition to lecturers, the training program design called for several leaders of small discussion groups. Although they would not present information, they would be required to have a good grasp of the information that would be presented. In addition, they would need a facility for encouraging teachers to examine their assumptions and to develop a better understanding of the background and point of view of the Mexican-American. The discussion leaders, in short, had to be bicultural. They were to be models for the teachers to resemble in teaching their own students. The discussion leaders had to demonstrate the sensitivities which the course was attempting to develop in the teachers. This required knowledge both of the problems the teachers faced in the classroom and of the problems faced by the minorities. Needless to say, the task of finding suitable discussion leaders was one of the most difficult aspects of the program development. When they could be located, they were often too committed to other tasks to be able to afford the time which the program required. Those who were finally hired included Richard Rios, a Chicano leader active statewide at the junior college and high school level; Yervant Andelian, a senior teacher-supervisor of Armenian descent who also taught Spanish as a second language; and Arthur Lopez, a junior high school vice-principal. Each of the discussion leaders could have presented information on the topics discussed. They were bilingual; they understood the problems faced by the classroom teacher; they embodied the sensitivities which it was hoped the teachers would begin to develop through participation in the course.

Another requisite for the course consisted of reading and reference materials that the teacher could consult for additional background information. The reading had to be current: figures, statistics, and issues would have to be of more than historical interest. At the same time, the reading would have to contain enough historical and cultural information for the teacher to gain a perspective on the current issues. The books and materials finally chosen were ones recommended by practitioners. Recommendations were from the interviews during the summer fieldwork.

RECRUITMENT, SELECTION, AND PLACEMENT OF PARTICIPANTS

Once the approval of each participating district had been obtained, a tentative course outline and an application form were sent to each teacher through the official summer mailing to teachers from the District offices. An enclosed letter mentioned that arrangements were being made for the course to be accredited through the State University Extension Service. The tuition charged for the course would be used to defray costs of the guest lecturers, discussion leaders, and printed materials.

Out of a total of some 1200 teachers contacted, 113 (approximately 11 percent) returned the application forms by the end of August. A pretest questionnaire was then mailed to each of the 113 with instructions to complete the questionnaire and return it before the commencement of school.

Ninety-eight teachers returned usable questionnaires. Using the information contained on the application form, teachers were matched according to specialization, years of teaching experience, previous contact with disadvantaged children, and district. They were then randomly allocated to two courses, one which was to begin in September and the other, its replication, in January. (The procedures used to form the two groups are detailed in Appendix A.) Teachers were notified at the beginning of the school year of the group in which they had been placed. In some instances, teachers expressed a preference for group placement. One teacher, for example, was getting married and thought she would have more time in the winter. Another had changed schools and needed to spend more time the first quarter on lesson preparation. The tuition fee was mentioned by some as a reason for being unable to take the autumn course. Others used the same explanation for dropping the course.*

---

*During the first week of school, it became apparent from conversations with teachers who had

DESCRIPTION OF THE TRAINING PROGRAM

Goals

The goals of the course were to increase the teacher's understanding of the cultural background of the Mexican-American child, and to help the teacher find ways to increase the child's self-esteem. The goals would be accomplished, it was felt, if teachers who participated became aware of their cultural blinders--their own assumptions--and became more concerned to learn about the cultural backgrounds of all their youngsters, not just Mexican-Americans. It was hoped that teachers would begin to differentiate among the types of learning problems the children were having, such as learning English as a second language.

Procedures

The course consisted of ten three-hour evening sessions held in a local school. Each session had three parts: (1) Lecture; (2) Question-and-answer period, followed by a coffee break; and (3) Discussion groups.

Lectures

Six Mexican-American community leaders and three Anglo educators presented information to the teachers

---

enrolled in the course that the tuition expenses, which had been increased to $50, were greater than many were willing to pay. An enrollment of fifty teachers was required to meet the terms of the agreement with the accrediting university. Rather than risk the collapse of the summer's efforts, and to demonstrate its commitment to the endeavor, the Whisman School District agreed to support the program financially by sharing the tuition costs, up to $2,500. It was hoped that other districts might also share the cost, but they had policy reasons for not doing so. As a result, many teachers from the associated districts decided to drop the course. Through an intensive recruitment program carried out primarily by the Curriculum Director of the Whisman School District with the assistance of teachers and administrators in the associated districts, enough teachers were found to meet the minimum requirements.

on the topics listed below. Each topic was related to the background factors influencing the Mexican-American, and each contributed to giving the teachers a view of the reality existing outside the school:

1. Introduction to Intercultural Studies
2. Mexican-American Organizations
3. The Struggle for Improvement of Labor Conditions
4. Latin Cultural Values: Cultural Differences
5. Latin Cultural Values: Religion and the Family
6. Problems Encountered by Spanish-Speaking Children Learning English
7. Home Visitations
8. Techniques for Developing Student Participation in the Classroom
9. Value Conflicts Between the Mexican-American Child and the School

Question-and-Answer Sessions

The question-and-answer sessions were intended to allow the teachers to pursue topics raised by the speaker and, through a dialogue, to become better acquainted with the speaker's point of view.

Discussion Groups

The discussion groups were designed to help the teacher relate what was discussed to the classroom. Another purpose of the discussion group was to build a climate of encouragement which would motivate the teacher to undertake a visit to the home of one or more of her Mexican-American children.

Field Experience

A home-visit exercise was introduced to bring teachers in closer touch with the families of the Mexican-American community.

POSTTEST

The posttest was administered by mail, as was the pretest. The questionnaire was mailed to both the treatment and comparison groups. Participants who were slow to respond were contacted by telephone and reminded to complete the questionnaire. When returned questionnaires were incomplete, teachers were contacted by telephone for their responses to the missing items.

REPLICATION

At the completion of the first program, participants were asked to suggest ways to improve subsequent course offerings.

Recommendations dealt primarily with the procedures used in the course. Regarding the speakers, some teachers asked for less militancy. A few recommended confrontation with students as well as adults. Some thought the speakers who gave concrete suggestions for ready adaptation to the classroom were best. Several requested more specific help for the classroom teacher than the course provided. Several teachers thought the speakers should start on time.

There were a number of recommendations regarding the discussion groups. Several complained that the discussion group seemed to drag at times and lacked direction. Some thought there should be more discussion of factual material and less time spent on opinions. Grouping teachers from different grade levels in the same discussion group was thought by several to be inadvisable. Some recommended rotating discussion group leaders or allowing discussion group members to rotate.

The recommendations were then interpreted by the researcher and screened. The chief screening criterion was whether the advice would enhance the experience of encountering another culture, which the course provided. The suggestion that the meetings "begin on time" was interpreted as a request to conform more closely to "Anglo" time as opposed to "Latin" time. The comments that the course "dragged" were taken seriously since it was not one of the objectives to bore the teachers.

The principal modification was procedural. During the replication, Spanish songs were taught during the first fifteen or twenty minutes of the evening. In this way, those who came on "Anglo" time were not penalized, and the introduction to a different way of looking at time was accomplished more comfortably, with less drag. Other suggestions, while useful, were not adopted due to the researcher's intention to keep the replication as much like the first course as possible. Thus, for example, the format of nonrotating discussion groups was adhered to rather than changing to one of rotating either discussion group leaders or members.

There were a whole host of factors which were not controllable. These factors make any type of field experiment hazardous, to say the least. Included would be other activities competing for teacher time; critical incidents in the community, which provided input into the discussions; the availability of discussion leaders; the moods and other commitments of the guest speakers; what was actually taking place from day to day in the teachers' own classrooms; discussions in teacher rooms in the various schools; events in the family causing absences, such as marriage, death, trips, and birthdays. In terms of the effect of these factors on the research design, what the researcher must do is assume that the uncontrolled influences were randomly distributed across both treatment and comparison groups. Being aware of these factors helps the person conducting field research to keep a flexible attitude toward events that are likely to occur in the field, but there is no satisfactory protection against them. Understanding the factors may help explain behavior which would otherwise be puzzling and perhaps annoying.

SECOND POSTTEST

The second posttest was handled as the pretest and first posttest had been, with two exceptions. Only those who took the second program took the second posttest. Secondly, there was less elapsed time between the conclusion of the second training program and the administration of the second posttest. Two months were allowed to elapse between the conclusion of the first training program and administration of the posttest.

TEACHER INTERVIEWS

At the conclusion of the two training programs, representative participants were interviewed, including some teachers who had dropped out before taking the training. Interviews were recorded, transcribed, and studied for influences the course may have had which were not reflected in the questionnaire data.

CHAPTER

4

ANALYSIS

REFINEMENT OF THE MEASURING INSTRUMENT

Subscale Formation, Reliability, and Validity

Factor analysis was used to generate subscales from the questionnaire data. The biomedical computer program was used to perform a principal component solution and an orthogonal rotation of the factor matrix (Dixon 1968: 169). Several runs were made with the data by varying the number of factor rotations. After each rotation, the items contributing to the various factors were examined for content in order to detect any underlying attitudinal continua. Eight subscales were discovered in this manner--four subscales belonging to the optimism dimension and four to the tolerance dimension.*

In terms of reliability, the subscales identified exhibited a range of Cronbach alpha coefficients from .10 to .70.** Four scales were dropped from the

---

*(F. Jonsson 1968: D-4) I later learned that the four subscales identified for the optimism dimension corresponded to the subscales intentionally developed by the author of the scale; whereas the discovery of four subscales for the tolerance dimension was a refinement which the author of the scale had not suspected.

**Cronbach alpha (Mehrens and Ebel 1967: 134):

$\alpha = \frac{n}{n-1}\left(1 - \sum_i V_i/V_t\right)$ = reliability coefficient,

where

n = No. of items,

$\sum_i V_i$ = sum of variance of each item,

V_t = variance of the scale.

analysis because of their relatively low alpha coefficient (less than .60). A fifth scale was excluded since it consisted of only one item. Of the three remaining scales, two were related to the tolerance dimension and one to the optimism dimension. The tolerance scale selected was one which was thought to be least affected by the grade which the teacher taught. Using it made it more reasonable to compare teacher scores across grade levels.

The tolerance scale consisted of the following five items from the questionnaire:

11. Mexican-American militancy causes an acceleration of progress toward social justice.

20. In the long run, humility and cooperativeness will serve the disadvantaged person better than aggressiveness and bravado.

48. Teachers of disadvantaged pupils should convey the attitude that use of demonstrations and boycotts is constructive and justifiable in the interests of improved life conditions for disadvantaged groups.

72. Even if Mexican-American militancy is a misguided concept or ideology, it has at least temporary utility in the fight for social justice.

81. If disadvantaged groups, especially as defined by ethnic or racial criteria, are to improve their lot as a whole, they must stand together and assert their demands as a group.

Based on analysis of the ninety-eight returns on the pretest, the reliability of this scale, using the Cronbach alpha coefficient, was .70.

The validity of the scale was determined by analyzing the reactions to the course of people who scored low on the scale. Data supplied by the course participant was augmented by anecdotal information gathered from students and classroom observation and interviews with teachers after the course. Respondents who scored relatively low on the scale tended to view the militant movement in negative terms, as doing more harm than good to the cause of improving the Mexican-American's situation. Those who scored relatively high on the scale tended to view the movement as a positive force that brought needed attention to the problems of the group.

The optimism scale was formed from the following items:

1. Disadvantaged family background places a "ceiling" on a child's achievement potential.

4. If a child has consistently had unsuccessful learning experiences in the primary grades, it is practically impossible to motivate him to learn in the intermediate grades.

13. Most of the improvements in the status of Mexican-Americans must be brought about through the efforts of socially concerned whites.

19. A child will respond well only to a teacher who is like the sort of adult the child hopes to become.

29. Few children are permanently failure-prone due to prior experience and background.

56. Even children with superior native ability can be so damaged by early environmental influences that they are virtually unteachable.

59. A child's preschool environment and experiences largely determine the later limits of his school achievement.

76. Whether a child achieves his full intellectual potential depends primarily on his relationships and experiences outside of school.

The reliability coefficient of the optimism scale is .63. Scale validity was determined using the same procedures described for the tolerance scale. Those who were low on the scale tended to view the out-of-school environment of the Mexican-American in negative terms. It was seen to impose serious limitations on the child's potential to achieve in school. Those who were high on the scale tended to view early environmental influence as a factor which did not necessarily limit the child's achievement potential.

In order to discover whether scale scores related in any way to observable teacher behavior in the classroom and patterns of teacher-student interaction, thirty-six teachers were observed in their classrooms after the conclusion of the second training program.* Thirty-two teachers were visited by the researcher. Andrew Cohen, doctoral candidate in Stanford's International Development Education Center conducted thirteen observations, which included nine of the teachers visited by the author.** Where there were disagreements in observation ratings, the two sets were averaged. The nonparametric correlations of observed behavior with the posttest scale scores of

---

*The observation form used was modeled after the Classroom Observation Record used in Ryans' teacher characteristics study. (Ryans 1960: 86). (See Appendix C.)

**This additional research, which substantially added to the credibility of the findings, was made possible by a grant from the Proctor and Gamble Fund, through the courtesy of Dr. A. P. Coladarci, Stanford University.

the teachers are shown in Table 1. Chi squares were run on each of the correlations.

The correlations do not indicate a significant relationship between the optimism dimension and teacher behavior or student behavior.

The tolerance dimension is shown to be significantly associated with two of the student behavior dimensions and one of the teacher behavior dimensions.

Teachers who scored high on tolerance were seen to have students who were more confident and more self-directed than teachers who scored low on the tolerance scale. Teachers who scored high on the tolerance scale were seen to associate more with the students than teachers who had scored low on the tolerance scale.

The relationships between teacher behavior, classroom variables, and student behavior are shown in Table 2.

Four of the teacher behavior variables were significantly correlated with grade level. Two of the teacher behavior variables were each significantly correlated with a student behavior variable.

Teachers were seen to become less understanding and more impatient as the grade level increased. Students of teachers who were patient or understanding tended to be more alert, whereas pupils of teachers who were impatient were seen as more withdrawn. It appeared that as grade level increased, the Mexican-American children were seen to be more withdrawn, less alert, and the teachers were seen to be increasingly impatient. As grade level increased, teachers were also seen to be more partial, more conformity oriented and more temperamental.

Teachers who were high in associatedness had students who appeared to be self-directed. Where the teacher was seen to be professional, the students were more likely to be dependent. Since the former teachers were also the ones who scored high on the tolerance scale, it seems possible to attribute to those with high tolerance a positive attitude toward the Mexican-American. This attitude is perceived by the child and reflected in his more outgoing, self-directed manner.

Formation of a Typology of Teacher Orientation

How the variables were related was treated as an empirical question rather than one to be settled *a priori*. At the conclusion of the project, the two scales were studied to determine the extent to which different levels of each variable could be labeled in

TABLE 1

Nonparametric Correlations of Background Variables, Student Behavior, and Teacher Behavior, with Attitude Scores of Participating Teachers
(N = 36)

Dimension	Tolerance	Optimism
Teacher Background Variables		
Sex	-.15	.01
Grade level	-.20	.11
Size of class	-.06	.16
Number of Mexican-Americans	-.10	.03
Observer ratings	-.00	-.14
Student Behavior (Mexican-American)		
Alterness	.19	.04
Cooperativeness	.25	.07
Confidence	.40[a]	.15
Self-directedness	.31[b]	.10
Teacher Behavior		
Patience	.23	.13
Flexibility	.11	.08
Relaxedness	-.01	-.10
Fairness	.20	.13
Diversity	.14	.02
Steadiness	.18	.01
Warmth	.19	.19
Involvement	.14	.18
Respectfulness	.26	.14
Associatedness	.25[a]	.19
Supportiveness	.13	.12

[a]Chi square significant at <.05> .01.

[b]Chi square significant at <.01.

Table 2

Nonparametric Correlations of Teacher Behavior with Classroom Variables and Student Behavior (N = 36)

Teacher Behavior	Classroom Variables					Student Behavior (Mexican-American)			
	Sex	Grade Level	Class Size	No. of Mex.-Am.	Observ. Ratings	Alert-ness	Cooper-ative-ness	Confi-dence	Self-direct-edness
Patience	-.08	-.32[a]	-.18	.12	.05	.38[a]	.17	.08	.23
Flexibility	.18	-.23	-.08	.19	.01	.12	-.02	-.08	.06
Relaxedness	.08	-.20	.01	.11	-.08	.06	.03	-.13	.01
Fairness	.01	-.36[a]	-.08	.04	.03	.13	-.08	.07	.08
Diversity	-.07	-.34[a]	-.02	.31	.14	.21	.04	.00	.12
Steadiness	-.06	-.38[a]	-.14	-.00	.03	.27	.21	.15	.15
Warmth	-.05	-.08	.17	-.05	.05	.26	.18	.17	.29
Involvement	.03	-.10	.15	.24	.12	.25	.23	.09	.16
Respectfulness	-.06	-.21	-.03	.06	.16	.21	.18	.14	.18
Associatedness	-.11	-.02	.13	-.02	.14	.39	.31	.23	.37[b]
Supportiveness	.05	-.30	-.12	.08	-.13	.29	.08	.03	.11

[a]Chi square significant at <.05> .01.

[b]Chi square significant at <.01.

a way that would represent their different meanings. The process involved in arriving at the typology was a reflective-inductive one, in which observations and scale scores of teachers were sifted and reflected upon in order to arrive at labels which seemed to do justice to what the person said in conversations and which bore some relation to their relative positions on the scale.

The labels which were chosen to represent the different levels of the dimension of optimism are pessimistic, realistic, and idealistic, for levels of low, medium, and high optimism.

The labels have been defined as follows:

<u>Pessimistic</u>: The out-of-school environment places irremediable handicaps on the potential of the Mexican-American child to achieve in school.

<u>Realistic</u>: The out-of-school environment imposes handicaps, but with proper attention, the child can overcome a large portion of the handicaps and achieve as a normal child.

<u>Idealistic</u>: Every child possesses similar ability and potential, regardless of background.

The labels chosen to represent different levels of the tolerance dimension are conservative, moderate, and liberal, with respect to their attitudes toward social change:

<u>Conservative</u>: The militant movement is a negative force; it does more harm than good. The idea of the American dream, the self-made man, describes how people rise. We should return to things as they used to be.

<u>Moderate</u>: The ideas of the militant movement are not as accurate as those of the Protestant work-ethic.

<u>Liberal</u>: The militant viewpoint is correct. Social change is necessary to meet the demands of the militants.

The combination of levels of optimism and tolerance are represented by the nine cells in Figure 2.

Each scale was marked in thirds, and the resulting grid was superimposed on the scatterplot, with the results represented in Figure 3. In this figure it is evident that the group of teachers is concentrated in the area labeled "Realistic Moderate." The next most concentrated cell is labeled "Idealistic Moderate."

The distribution of scores--biased toward the upper end of the optimism scale--is what one would expect, owing to the self-selection factor, since only interested teachers returned completed pretests.

FIGURE 2

Typology of Teacher Orientation

TOLERANCE SCALE	Pessimistic (Low)	Realistic (Medium)	Idealistic (High)
Liberal (High)	Pessimistic Liberal	Realistic Liberal	Idealistic Liberal
Moderate (Medium)	Pessimistic Moderate	Realistic Moderate	Idealistic Moderate
Conservative (Low)	Pessimistic Conservative	Realistic Conservative	Idealistic Conservative

O P T I M I S M S C A L E

THE RESEARCH HYPOTHESES

The following hypotheses are to be tested:

H.1. Previous experience with disadvantaged students will affect the pretest tolerance and optimism scores. Direction not specified.

H.2. Teachers exposed to the status quo will exhibit a negative change on the tolerance dimension and/or the optimism dimension. Teachers exposed to the supplementary training program, on the other hand, will not experience a negative change in attitude.

H.3. The direction of change produced in the first training program will be replicated in the second training program.

TESTS OF THE HYPOTHESES

C.1.1. Test of First Hypothesis: Controlling for Length of Teaching Experience

> H.1. Previous experience with disadvantaged students will affect the pretest tolerance and optimism scores. Direction not specified.

FIGURE 3

Scatterplot of Teacher Pretest Scores Located on the Typology of Teacher Orientation

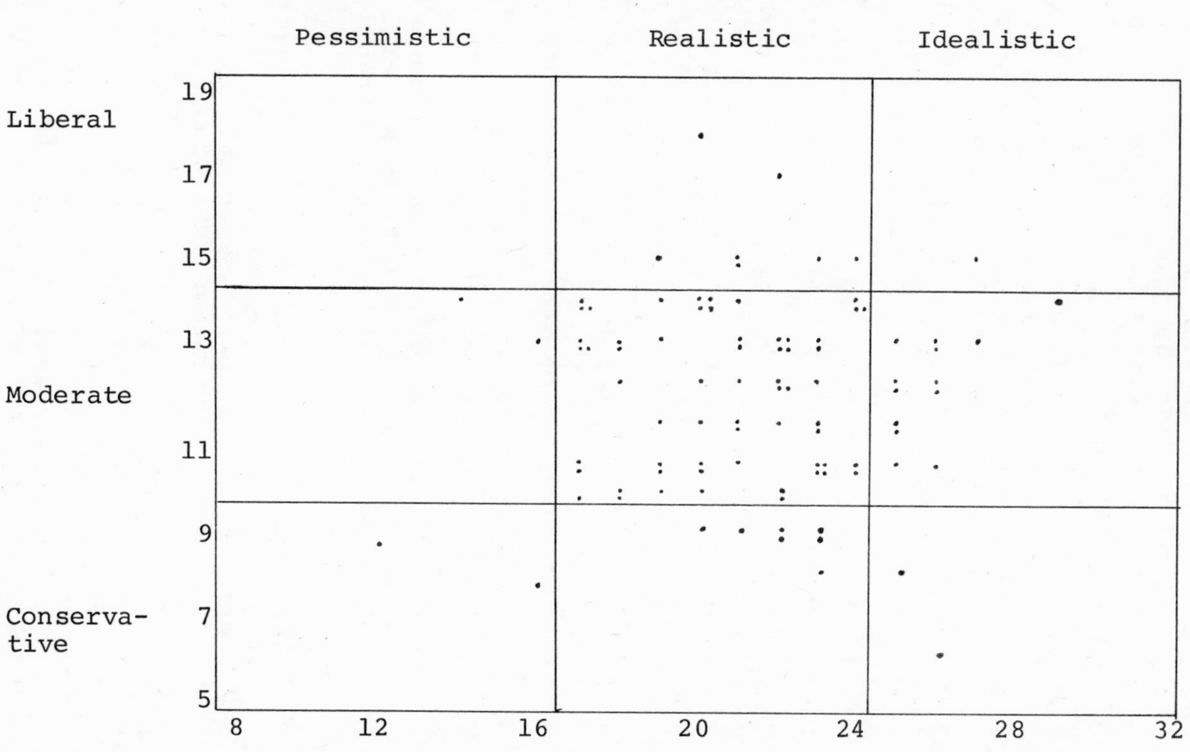

Through an analysis of the pretest data, different levels of optimism and tolerance were expected to appear among those teachers having different amounts of previous teaching experience as well as different amounts of experience with disadvantaged children.

In order to test the relationships, teachers who were new to their district were placed in one category, teachers with from one to six years of experience were placed in another, and teachers with seven or more years of experience in the district in a third. The principal reason for subdividing teachers into these groups was the pragmatic need for cell entries of sufficient size for statistical analysis. The grouping allowed for comparisons among new teachers, teachers with intermediate experience in the district, and teachers who were relatively established in the district.

Each subgroup thus formed was again subdivided on the basis of reported experience with disadvantaged children. Teachers with less than a year of experience were placed in one group, and those with a year or more of experience were placed in another. Cross tabulations were used to determine significant differences among the subgroups with respect to their initial levels of tolerance and optimism.*

When the length of teaching experience in the district was controlled for, previous experience with disadvantaged children was not significantly related to initial levels of tolerance or optimism.

C.1.2. Test of First Hypothesis: Controlling for Experience with Disadvantaged

> H.1. Previous experience with disadvantaged students will affect the pretest tolerance and optimism scores. Direction not specified.

This part of the test of the first hypothesis is designed to detect differences among teachers with different levels of experience in the district when experience with disadvantaged children is controlled for. (The information pertaining to the analysis is presented in Tables 3 and 4.)

---

*The chi square analysis was performed by dichotomizing each level of experience within the district at the median for that level. The analysis was performed using the SPSS FASTAB program.

TABLE 3

Pretest Tolerance Score Frequencies of Teachers by Experience with Disadvantaged Children and Length of Teaching Experience in the District (N = 98)

Years with Disadvantaged	Median Indicator	Years in District 0	1-6	7+	Chi Square	Significance Level
1 or less (Md = 13.38)	>Md	6	6	4	3.33	n.s.
	<Md	11	5	1		
Over 1 (Md = 12.94)	>Md	5	17	14	.001	n.s.
	<Md	4	14	11		

There were no significant differences among teachers on the tolerance scale (Table 3). However, Table 4 reveals significant differences in levels of optimism when teachers of the three levels of teaching experience are compared, who have all had at least a year of experience with disadvantaged children.

The relative percentages of teachers who scored above the median in optimism, given that they had at least a year of experience with the disadvantaged, were 44 percent, 74 percent, and 36 percent for teachers beginning in the district, with one to six years of experience in the district, and over seven years of experience in the district, respectively.

Figure 4 illustrates the significant difference between the optimism of teachers with one to six years in the district who have had at least one year of experience with disadvantaged children, and the other two groups of teachers. Another feature brought out in the figure is the remarkable similarity of the medians on the tolerance scale of teachers at the three levels of teaching experience who have had a year or more of experience with disadvantaged children.

TABLE 4

Pretest Optimism Score Frequencies of Teachers
by Experience with Disadvantaged Children
and Length of Teaching Experience
in the District
(N = 98)

Years with Disadvantaged	Median Indicator	Years in District 0	1-6	7+	Chi Square	Significance Level
1 or less (Md = 20.60)	>Md	9	5	3	.32	n.s.
	<Md	8	6	2		
Over 1 (Md = 21.85)	>Md	4	23	9	8.68[a]	.01
	<Md	5	8	16		

[a]Chi square between teachers with one to six years of experience and those with seven or more equals 6.7, which is significant at <.01. Chi square between teachers with one to six years of experience, and teachers beginning in the district equals 4.2, which is significant at <.05.

On the basis of the data in Tables 3 and 4, two refined hypotheses are proposed:

H.1.1. In elementary school districts characterized by a student population in which 13-20 percent of the children come from backgrounds perceived by the teachers to be disadvantaged, teachers who are new to the district will more frequently be lower in tolerance than teachers who have had several years of experience in the district, given that both groups of teachers have had less than a year's experience with disadvantaged children.

H.1.2. In elementary school districts with a student population in which 13-20 percent of the children come from backgrounds perceived by the teachers

FIGURE 4

Cross-Sectional Data Representing Three Different Levels of Experience Within the District, Each Level Being Further Subdivided to Reflect Two Levels of Experience with Disadvantaged Children

(Experience levels are indicated by the numbers on the figure. Arrow tips mark the median score of teachers in that group with a year or more of experience with minority and/or poor children. Arrow feathers mark the median scores of teachers with less than a year's experience with minority and/or poor children.)

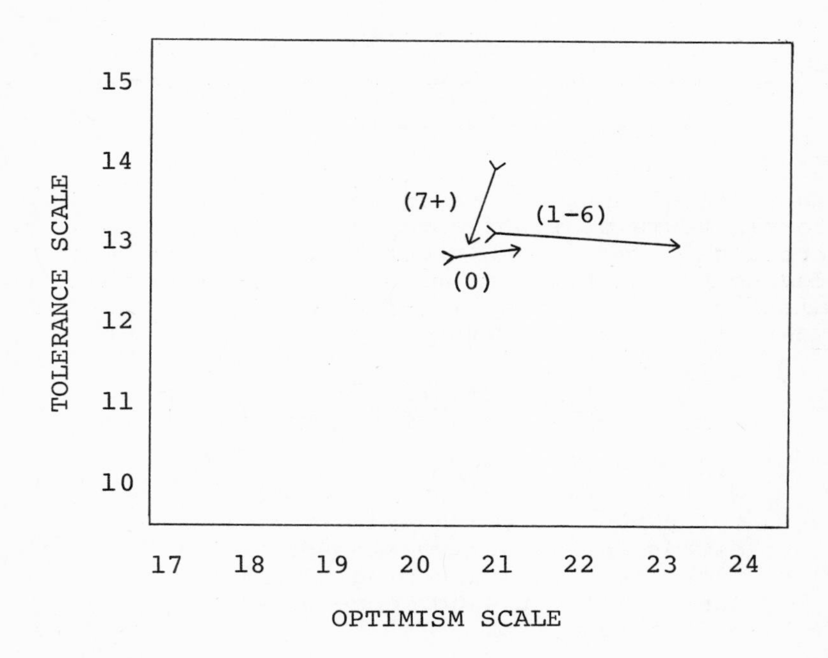

TABLE 5

Comparison of Median Scores of Teachers Arranged by Years of Experience and Experience with Disadvantaged[a]

	Experience with Disadvantaged Children					
	1 Year or More			Less than 1 Year		
Years in District	Tolerance	Optimism	n	Tolerance	Optimism	n
0	12.9	20.4	17	13.0	21.3	9
1-6	13.2	20.8	11	13.0	23.2	31
7+	14.0	20.9	5	12.9	20.6	25

[a]Pretest data graphed in Figure 4.

to be disadvantaged, teachers who have had from one to six years of experience in the district will more frequently be higher in optimism than new teachers or teachers with seven or more years of experience in the district, given that all teachers have had at least a year of experience with disadvantaged children.

C.2.1. Test of Second Hypothesis: Analysis of Changes in Matched Groups

> H.2. Teachers exposed to the status quo will exhibit a negative change on the tolerance dimension and/or the optimism dimension. Teachers exposed to the supplementary training program, on the other hand, will not experience a negative change of attitude.

In order to compare the effects of training against the effect of the status quo on teacher tolerance and optimism, teachers who completed pretest, posttest, and training course were matched with teachers who completed pretest and posttest but not the course. The procedure used for matching the individuals is presented in Appendix A, Section 2.

<u>Tolerance Dimension</u>. The data comparing the treatment group with the matched comparison group on the pretest and posttest are shown in Figure 5. The arrows reflect a tendency for the control group to become less tolerant and slightly less optimistic, while the treatment group moves toward a position of greater tolerance and higher optimism.

The arrows showing the shift in median scores for both variables on the pretest and posttest become more meaningful when interpreted by use of elementary vector analysis. (See Figure 6.) Each of the arrows indicating a change in median is considered a vector. The teachers in the comparison group are influenced by one vector, namely, the classroom vector (C). Teachers in the treatment group feel the influence of the course vector (T). However, the latter group also feels the force of the classroom vector (C). The arrow representing the outcome of change in the

FIGURE 5

Comparison Between Teachers Who Received Training with Teachers in the Comparison Group on the Pretest and Posttest

(Arrow tips represent posttest medians. Arrow feathers represent pretest medians.)

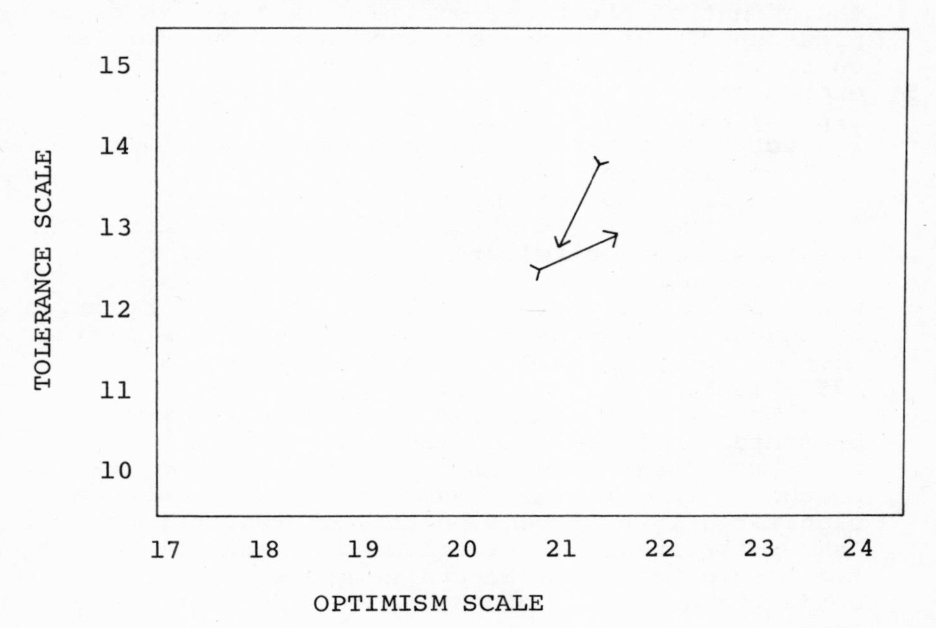

TABLE 6

Comparison of Median Scores of Teachers in the Treatment and Comparison Groups on the Pretest and Posttest

	Treatment Group (n = 28)		Matched Comparison Group (n = 28)	
	Tolerance	Optimism	Tolerance	Optimism
Pretest	12.5	21.0	13.7	21.7
Posttest	12.9	22.0	12.7	21.2

treatment group must therefore be the resultant vector (R) reflecting the effect of two forces working in somewhat opposite directions--the classroom vector and the treatment vector.

In Figure 6, vector (C) represents the "classroom effect." Vector (T) represents the "treatment effect," and vector (R) represents the resultant of both vectors (C) and (T). As shown in the figure, the effect of the classroom is in a negative or depressant direction on both variables, but more so on tolerance than on optimism, while the treatment exerts an effect in the opposite direction. What finally happens to teacher attitudes must of course reflect the operations of both the classroom vector and the treatment vector.

In order to determine the statistical significance of the changes, a comparison was made between treatment and control groups with respect to a net shift in each group above or below the median. The exact probability of this net shift having occurred by chance was computed by use of Tocher's modification of the Fisher Exact Probability Test (Siegel 1956: 102).

The data on which the test was performed are presented in Table 7 and Table 8.

It is seen from Table 7 that the directions of change in the treatment and comparison groups were significantly different on the tolerance dimension. As hypothesized, the direction of change among teachers exposed to the status quo was negative, while the direction of change among the teachers

FIGURE 6

Vector Diagram Representing Classroom Effect, Treatment Effect, and the Resultant for the Training Group

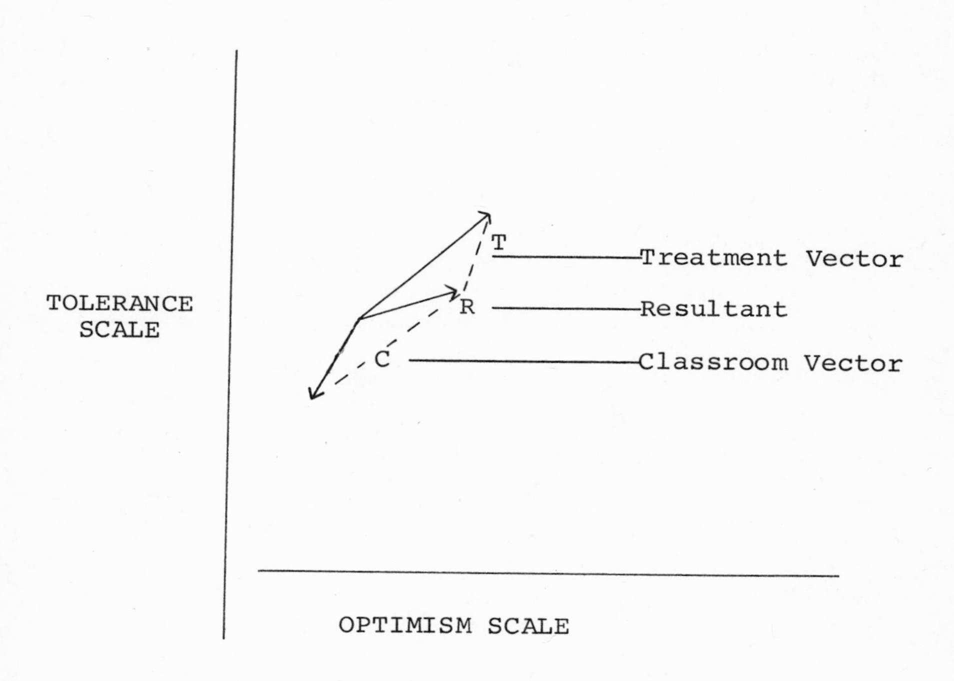

TABLE 7

Analysis of Shift or Direction of Change in Tolerance Scores for Teachers in the Treatment and Matched Comparison Groups

Teacher Group	Direction of Change: >Md on Pretest <Md on Posttest	Direction of Change: <Md on Pretest >Md on Posttest	Exact Probability
Treatment	0	5	
Matched Comparison	4	2	.047

receiving the supplementary training was slightly positive. It can be concluded that the status quo and the training program affected teacher tolerance in opposite directions.

When the changes are analyzed using the Fisher Exact Probability Test, the probability that the results shown in Table 8 could have occurred by chance is .08. This level of significance is low enough for us to reject the null hypothesis at the .1 level. The direction of change is the same as that noted for the tolerance scores.*

TABLE 8

Analysis of Shift or Direction of Change in Optimism Scores for Teachers in the Treatment and Matched Comparison Groups

Teacher Group	Direction of Change: >Md on Pretest <Md on Posttest	Direction of Change: <Md on Pretest >Md on Posttest	Exact Probability
Treatment	1	6	
Matched Comparison	4	2	.08

*The data were initially examined using the *t*-test. Significant posttest differences between the experimental and control groups were found for two of the three subgroups in our sample. (See next section.) After studying the data, however, I realized that the assumptions required for parametric statistics could not be satisfied. The scores did not conform to a normal distribution nor could I assume the scales permitted more than an ordinal scale of measurement. Since the *t*-test requires that the observations be measured at least in an interval scale, the *t*-test was not used (Siegel 1956: 35). It is interesting that both the *t*-test analysis and the nonparametric approach finally adopted supported similar conclusions.

C.2.2. Test of Second Hypothesis: Analysis of Changes Within Subgroups

> H.2. Teachers exposed to the status quo will exhibit a negative change on the tolerance dimension and/or the optimism dimension. Teachers exposed to the supplementary training program, on the other hand, will not experience a negative change of attitude.

This test of the second hypothesis considers each subgroup (defined by years of experience in the district) in an attempt to determine more precisely where the significant changes originated.

Tolerance Dimension. The data for the tolerance dimension are presented in Table 9.

Optimism Dimension. Turning now to the optimism dimension (Table 10), 54 percent of the teachers in the

TABLE 9

Comparison of Subgroups Within the Treatment and Matched Comparison Groups on the Pretest and Posttest--Tolerance Dimension

	Relationship to Median							
	Treatment				Comparison			
Years in District	Pretest <Md	Pretest >Md	Posttest <Md	Posttest >Md	Pretest <Md	Pretest >Md	Posttest <Md	Posttest >Md
0	4	3	3	4	3	4	4	3
1-6	7	5	5	7	5	7	7	5
7+	3	6	4	5	5	4	7	2
Chi Square	1.48		.02		.45		1.05	
Significance	n.s.		n.s.		n.s.		n.s.	

Note: None of the differences was significant at the .1 level or better.

treatment group scored above the median on the pretest. This increased to 71 percent on the posttest, for a net gain. The matched comparison group changed from 54 percent scoring above the median on the pretest to 46 percent on the posttest, for a net loss.

Looking at the pretest differences between the subgroups in the treatment group, 43 percent of the (0) teachers scored above the median, compared with 58 percent and 56 percent of the (1-6) and (7+) teachers. In the comparison group, the (0) and (1-6) teachers were significantly higher in optimism than the (7+) teachers. Of the (0) teachers, 71 percent scored above the median, while 75 percent of the (1-6) teachers and only 11 percent of the (7+) teachers scored above the median.

Considering the posttest, the differences in the treatment group were contributed by the teachers with over one year of experience in the district. The percentage of (0) teachers in the treatment group stayed the same (43 percent scored above the median). The percentage of (1-6) teachers scoring above the median increased from 58 percent to 75 percent, and that of (7+) teachers from 56 percent to 89 percent.

Considering the comparison group, the percentage of (0) teachers scoring above the median dropped from

TABLE 10

Comparison of Subgroups Within the Treatment and Matched Comparison Group on the Pretest and Posttest--Optimism Dimension

	Relationship to Median							
	Treatment				Comparison			
Years in District	Pretest <Md	Pretest >Md	Posttest <Md	Posttest >Md	Pretest <Md	Pretest >Md	Posttest <Md	Posttest >Md
0	4	3	4	3	2	5	3	4
1-6	5	7	3	9	3	9	5	7
7+	4	5	1	8	8	1	7	2
Chi Square	.45		4.22		9.64		3.13	
Significance	n.s.		.12		.01		n.s.	

75 percent to 57 percent. The percentage of (1-6) teachers in the comparison group who scored above the median dropped from 75 percent to 58 percent. In the (7+) group, there was a net increase of one teacher who scored above the median on the posttest. The same relative differences between the three subgroups persisted on the posttest, but they were less pronounced.

Summary of Subgroup Changes for Both Scales. The changes in the subgroup medians from the pretest to the posttest on both scales have been plotted in Figures 7 and 8 for the treatment and matched comparison groups, respectively.

The figures illustrate the significant differences in the direction of change for the treatment and comparison groups. While the subgroups in the comparison group uniformly drop in median scores, the medians of the two subgroups in the treatment group increase. The drop in tolerance noted in the (7+) group of teachers is less than the drop in tolerance recorded for the (7+) teachers in the comparison group.

Another point emphasized by the figures is the move toward greater concensus in the treatment group with respect to tolerance, which was not paralleled by the changes in the comparison group. On the posttest, the subgroups in the treatment group were more similar on the tolerance scale, as reflected by the medians.

Figure 7 reveals the similarity that existed between (7+) teachers on the one hand, versus the (0) teachers on the other, with respect to tolerance scores, both before and after the course. Figure 8, dealing with the comparison group, shows that in terms of optimism, the (0) teachers were more like the (1-6) teachers and the (7+) teachers formed a subgroup that was distinctly lower in optimism than the other two groups.

The data support the hypothesis that the second course influenced teachers in the same direction as the first course with respect to the optimism dimension. One may conclude that courses of this type have a predictable effect on teacher tolerance, but not on teacher optimism.

C.3. Test of Third Hypothesis

> H.3. The direction of change produced in the first training program will be reproduced in the second training program.

FIGURE 7

Comparison of the Three Subgroups of Teachers in the Treatment Group on the Pretest and Posttest

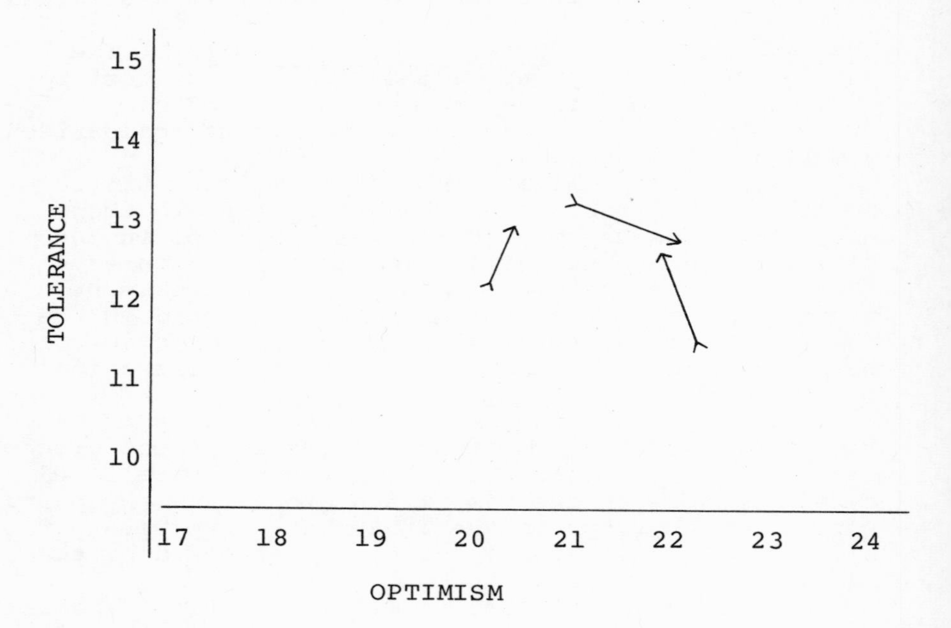

TABLE 11

Median Scores for Treatment Group Arranged by Years of Experience in District

Years in District	Tolerance Pretest	Tolerance Posttest	Optimism Pretest	Optimism Posttest
0 (n = 7)	12.3	13.0	20.0	20.3
1-6 (n = 12)	11.5	12.8	22.5	22.0
7+ (n = 9)	13.3	12.8	21.0	22.3

FIGURE 8

Comparison of the Three Subgroups of Teachers in the Matched Comparison Group on the Pretest and Posttest

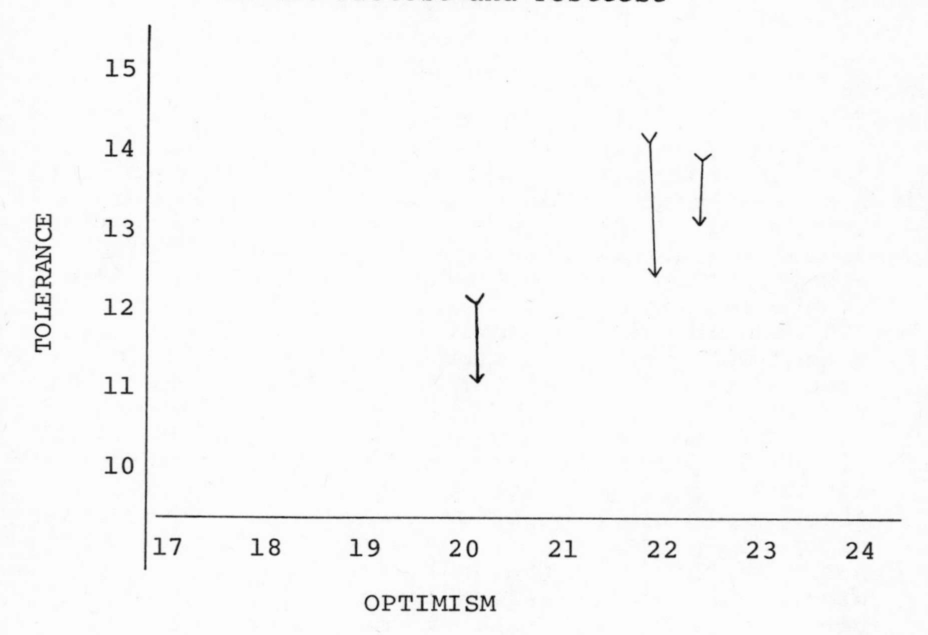

TABLE 12

Median Scores for Matched Comparison Group Arranged by Years of Experience in District

Years in District	Tolerance Pretest	Tolerance Posttest	Optimism Pretest	Optimism Posttest
0 (n = 7)	14.0	12.3	21.9	22.0
1-6 (n = 12)	13.8	13.0	22.5	22.5
7+ (n = 9)	12.0	11.0	19.8	19.8

The test of the hypothesis is based on an analysis of the scores of nineteen teachers who completed the pretest and both posttests.

The median scores on each scale are presented in Table 13 and charted in Figure 9.

UNMEASURED ASPECTS OF THE TRAINING PROGRAM

Method

After the completion of both training programs, forty-eight of the participants were given open-ended interviews. Each interview was held at the teacher's school and taped, with the teacher's permission. Sixty-three percent of the interviews were conducted by the researcher's assistant, and the remainder, by the researcher. Transcriptions of the interviews together with written course evaluation statements were studied in order to determine major outcomes of the course.

In order to provide a framework for the interviews, a cybernetic model of the educational process was developed, and each component of the model was transposed into a question. The questions probed the teacher's perception of the behavior of her Mexican-American children, the goals for their learning, the procedures used to assist learning, the assumptions behind those procedures, the methods of evaluating student progress, the teacher's understanding of background factors influencing student behavior, and modifications in her approach resulting from the course. (The model developed as a basis for the questions appears in Appendix E.)

The data were then studied to arrive at answers to two questions:

1. Which elements of the cybernetic model of the educational process were most affected by the training program?
2. What process was involved in fostering change?

Effects of the Training Program

The training program primarily affected three elements of the cybernetic model: the teacher's perception of the background factors influencing student behavior, her perception of the nature of the problem

FIGURE 9

Comparison of the Scores for the Group of Teachers Taking the Second Training Program

(Chart of median scores reported in Table 13.)

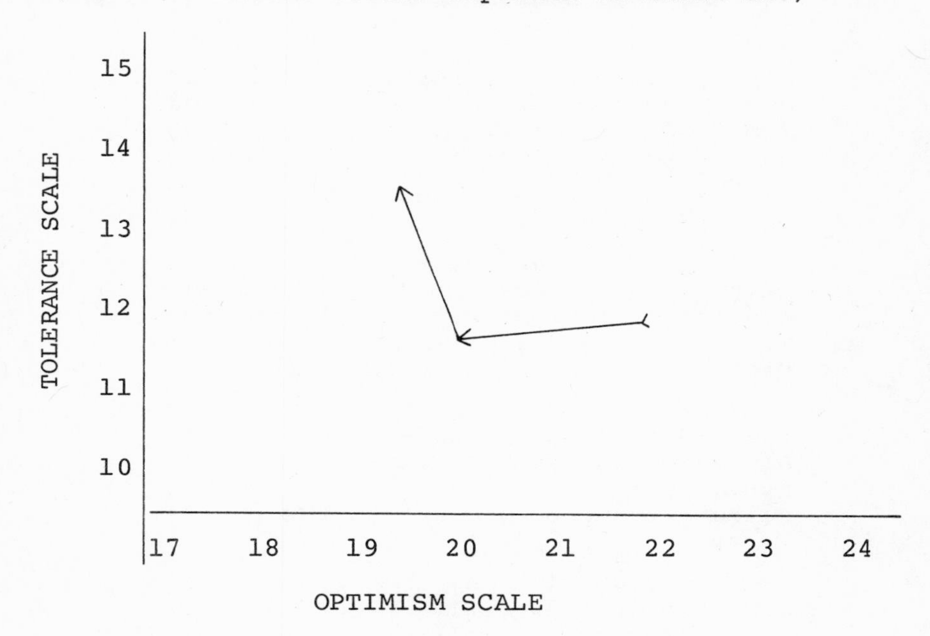

TABLE 13

Median Scores on the Pretest and First and Second Posttests for Teachers in the Second Training Program (N = 19)

	Pretest	First Posttest	Second Posttest
Tolerance	11.85	11.67	13.58
Optimism	21.67	19.75	19.00

area, and her understanding of alternative procedures (approaches and strategies) for improving the learning situation.

A number of the participants, especially the new teachers, were made aware of the existence of the Mexican-American community and the fact of intergroup hostility. The following comments were all made by teachers who were beginning their teaching in the district:

> I came here in September and didn't even know the Mexican-American existed. I'm from [out-of-state] and there just aren't Mexican-American people there.
>
> You don't read about them in the papers, and you don't hear about them.
>
> I really was unaware of the gravity of any problems as far as the Mexican-American relations with the white community, because I'm from . . . and I just didn't know there was such a problem.
>
> I picked up many generalizations that just helped me understand Latin American culture from many of the speakers. . . . They were an unknown culture to me before I took the course.
>
> It was never in my experience to have contact with any [Mexican-Americans] directly or indirectly. I didn't even know there was a problem until I came to live in California, which was just four months ago.

The comments of the beginning teachers reflect an initial lack of knowledge about their Mexican-American children, which may be characteristic of teachers coming from out-of-state who have had little contact with the Mexican-American group. For these teachers, an effect of the course was to make them more aware of the heterogeneous cultural backgrounds of the youngsters with whom they were working in the classroom, and in particular, aware of the existence of the Mexican-American. The lack of awareness was not limited to teachers who had come to the area from out-of-state, as illustrated by the following comment:

> I was born in this area and I didn't really realize, until I had taken this

> course, that there were any conflicts in this area. I had always thought of them as being part of the community, and hadn't realized that they were being left out of anything. . . .

An increased awareness of the Mexican-American culture was not limited to beginning teachers. More experienced teachers also mentioned that the course took them further than they had been before. For example, one teacher commented:

> I haven't really been studying Mexican-American culture as deeply as it was presented in the course. Superficially, I can be sympathetic to any race, nationality, or culture, and I am able to adjust quite easily to the differences and be quite comfortable with the Japanese or the Koreans, or the Spanish or the Americans--but I never studied the background to find the kernel of the ideas behind all this.

For some teachers, it was a revelation to learn that the Mexican-American was not a newcomer in California. The following statement drives home the extent to which at least one teacher was moved by the knowledge that the Mexican-American has every claim to the rights of citizenship:

> I had believed that all Mexican-Americans were poor farm workers, mostly transient, and all lazy and ignorant. I thought they shouldn't complain, since they had chosen the U.S. over Mexico--we didn't bring them, and they could always leave. I now realize that these people are not <u>Mexican-Americans</u>, but <u>Americans</u>! Their families have been here for three generations or more. This was the biggest change in my thinking.
>
> And those whom I met Wednesday nights were educated, poised, and friendly--proving that ability and drive were there, but not being given a chance.

Another teacher commented on her greater appreciation for the work which the Mexican-Americans are doing to improve their situation. This teacher expressed a new awareness of the level of parental aspirations for their children:

> Before I began the course, I think there was a "generation gap" in my views about the Mexican-American. If I can generalize, I considered him to be a shy, passive, family-oriented individual, who accepted the obvious inequities in our culture, and was not striving for a better way of life. The image of the Mexican-American as a frustrated people who are beginning to use political means to achieve a better way of life is new to me. I am beginning to sense some of the higher aspirations which they have for their children.

Many of the participants became aware of specific ways in which the cultural background of the Mexican-American differed from their own. Language differences, such as the greater number of sounds in English than Spanish, were mentioned. Teachers said they were helped by knowing about the emphasis on "being" rather than "doing." They became more aware of the Mexican-American's emphasis on loyalty and family pride, as opposed to a materialistic achievement orientation. One teacher said:

> I have become aware of their philosophy, "If God wills it," and this has changed my opinion about Mexican-Americans being lazy.

Teachers also became acquainted with ways in which the "silent language" could be used to explain certain behavior patterns. Teachers who insist that a child "look them in the eye" when being disciplined find it disconcerting when the Mexican-American child looks at the floor. According to a teacher with considerable experience in the district,

> I learned a great deal. . . . There were things that I didn't understand, especially like a child holding his head down for respect. This is very annoying when you don't understand this.

As teachers became more aware of the fact of cultural differences, they began to appreciate the negative effects these differences have on learning when they are not understood by the school:

> He [the Mexican-American child] values loyalty to family and peers, self-pride, manliness, and "being" someone rather than "doing" something. He probably feels that his own culture is inferior because it has been treated that way in the school society. This has resulted in a deep distrust of teachers and an effective mask of defenses that is difficult to penetrate. He has learned well to "play the game."

Awareness of differences helped teachers better understand the complexity of the problem. They saw their own approaches contributing to the difficulties:

> Before the course began, I felt somewhat defeated working with the Mexican-American families. I felt they did not move toward a standard of caring for children that I felt was important and necessary. Since the course on Mexican-American culture I have learned possibly my approach was wrong. I didn't take enough time to establish a helpful relationship with them. I didn't spend enough time searching for their real needs. . . . I feel now I have learned enough about the Mexican culture to talk with the parents of children in a more understanding and approachable manner.

Another teacher said that she had previously thought she treated all children just alike. The course influenced her to realize that by treating all children alike, regardless of background, she was in fact discriminating aginst the children who, because of their different background, were not familiar with the teacher's middle-class language, vocabulary, gestures and temperament. "I treated all children the same," she said, "actually ignoring the differences which I now feel should be pointed out and discussed in classes."

Teachers began to see the problem area in terms of misunderstandings and lack of knowledge about one another:

> The most important thing this course has done is to make me aware of how very

> little I know my students--all of them--
> and how little they probably know of me
> and how great is the need to know and
> understand one another.
>
> Through this course I have achieved
> a deeper understanding of how learning
> has been affected through misunderstand-
> ings of cultural differences. I believe
> I have developed an admiration for this
> minority group because of their patience
> with educators.

As teachers became more aware of the contrasts between the value systems of the Mexican-American culture and their own culture, they were better able to understand how the school experience could cause difficulties for the child. Teachers began to see that many difficulties stem from the misunderstandings arising from contact between two cultural groups. It became apparent that when teachers were unaware of the cultural differences, they were unable to play a mediating role in helping the Mexican-American child adjust to the classroom and in helping the Anglo children adjust to the Mexican-American children. Teachers found ways of modifying their approaches to mediate more effectively between the child's cultural background and the classroom situation. The following sums up the responses of several teachers:

> The course has provided a much more
> rounded understanding of their culture and
> the effect that this culture has on them
> today. The understanding of the family
> structure was indeed valuable since in my
> experience the father has not been seen
> at school as often as the mother. I also
> have further understanding for the mother
> who does not come to school because she
> speaks another language. When this situ-
> ation occurs, I realize as a teacher I
> have more alternatives, one of which would
> be a home visit, merely as a means of the
> parents to know me casually and perhaps
> remove the fear of school.
>
> I also feel more prepared to teach
> the culture of the Mexican-American be-
> cause I'm interested in learning more
> details of their history. They have an
> intriguing, rich background which I know
> only sketchily.

One of the most important of the new alternatives was the "positive" home visit: The teacher would visit to praise the child's progress rather than to point out failures in his performance:

> I also got a deep interest in the home visiting--just doing as much as I could. They were an unknown culture before I took the course.

Teachers benefitted not only from the home visits and from learning more about the reactions of other teachers to the visits, but also from other aspects of the course. The following quotation suggests the scope of what was gained and pinpoints the home visitations as being a critical aspect of the training program:

> I was grateful to hear what the speakers had to say, and was enchanted at hearing what other teachers at other levels had to say about how they feel, what they think, what they're doing, and what they recognize and what I feel they don't recognize. That was exciting for me, and I think this would not have occurred outside the course. It's something they don't talk about in the coffee rooms; but we did talk about it in the course. This was tremendously important. . . . I felt strongly when I came away from the course that home visits were vital.

THE PROCESS INVOLVED IN BRINGING ABOUT CHANGE

During the course of the research it was possible to form some opinions about the process involved in bringing about change. The sources of the opinions included discussions with teachers and administrators, observations, interviews with students, and recordings in a journal. The following discussion is impressionistic and theoretical.

Three elements were crucial for the development and maintenance of the training program: administrative support, militant pressure, and an action-research specialist. Power resides at the level of the superintendent, without whose support, the resources of the district would not have been made available for the project. Pressure from the militant minority leaders was important since it kept the school officials in a state of anxiety, in which they were open to new ideas and assistance from outside sources in order to meet militant demands. The demands of the minority leaders ensured that the training program would be perceived as relevant to the needs of the schools. An action-research specialist, in the role of program coordinator, was needed to bridge the gap between the school and community leaders. These three elements, working in mutual cooperation to improve school-community relations, formed the relational infrastructure for the project. It was possible to develop a training program to bring about changes in teachers' attitudes because of this infrastructure.

The process underlying the changes in the teachers was a form of the acculturation process whereby teachers' attitudes were modified through a series of planned exposures to Mexican-Americans and acculturated educators, in the direction of becoming more aware of the cultural background of the Mexican-American and the points of view associated with that background.

An element of the training program which fostered acculturation was sufficient time for the process to take place. Rather than a one-day conference with limited teacher participation, the course was extended over ten weeks. At each session the teachers were brought face-to-face with speakers from the other culture. Dialogue and interpersonal relationships were developed by means of the discussion groups, which were conducted in a supportive environment in which teachers were encouraged to be open about their feelings--both negative and positive--toward the speakers and the subjects they discussed.

It was assumed that in order to motivate teachers to change their normal perception patterns, some mild incongruity or dissonance would have to be introduced in the perceived interaction pattern between teacher and students. Otherwise, when advised to establish better communication with the Mexican-American community, the teacher might say, "Why bother? Things are perfectly all right as they are." On the other hand, if the dissonance created were too great, the teacher would be apt to turn off the source of dissonance, either by dropping the course or by adopting a hardened stance opposed to further efforts on behalf of the Mexican-American community. "It's up to them to change," a teacher might say, "not up to me. After all, this is America."

The strategy was to introduce a mild form of dissonance, sufficient to motivate the teacher to expand her awareness, but not so great as to be threatening or overpowering. Speakers in the first part of the course expressed hostility toward the educational system and made it clear that a human relations problem existed. Teachers were made aware of points of view different from their own. Through exposure to cultural background information, the teachers became more aware of contextual factors influencing the Mexican-American child. Greater knowledge of the religion, family structure, and language helped the teachers to realize the extent of their own ignorance about the subculture. At the same time, the increased knowledge helped build the teacher's self-confidence in relating with Mexican-American children and their families.

The teachers became aware of the incongruity between an acculturated teaching style and the ones which they were employing. This awareness motivated the teachers to seek further information from other speakers, the discussion groups, and home visits, in order to reduce the incongruity by learning how to relate in a more acculturated way to the Mexican-Americans. Teachers who were unable to regard an acculturated style as desirable did not experience an incongruity, since from their point of view, the onus of adjustment is on the Mexican-American.

Through the lectures the teachers were provided with approaches and strategies for increasing communication and dialogue between the teacher and the home. Teachers became more aware that they could increase the child's self-esteem in school by acknowledging and valuing his ability to speak Spanish, thereby adding to rather than subtracting from his cultural background. Teachers also became more aware of the extent to which their own attitudes and behavior in the classroom were culturally determined. For some it was the first time they had been made aware of the extent to which silent language, eye contact, for example, had to be modified for effective communication to take place.

An effect of increased awareness was a change in the array of assumptions which the teacher held about the Mexican-American. Assumptions about the structure of the family, for example, were altered by home visits. Assumptions about the way the Mexican-American child learned English were altered through learning more about the way a Spanish-speaking child _hears_ English.

Another effect of increased awareness was to help the teachers concentrate on areas of learning where they could do some good, such as learning English as a second language. They also acquired a better idea of specific things that could be done to improve the standing of Mexican-American children, such as finding substitutes for the "Anglo IQ" tests used for placement purposes.

In addition to becoming more aware of the background of the Mexican-American, the teachers became more conscious of their own points of view. Teachers recognized how some of their attitudes and behavior could impede communication with the children and some planned for continued steps in the acculturation process by enrolling in a Spanish conversation course.

Summing up, the information provided by the speakers and through the discussion groups influenced the teachers' perceptions of the normative approach to be used with Mexican-American children. This influence was at the cognitive and affective level. Over time, where the influence was sufficiently strong, the teacher was affected at the psychomotor level, and old habit patterns were modified in an acculturative direction.

CHAPTER

5

RESULTS, CONCLUSIONS, AND RECOMMENDATIONS

METHOD

The research was consciously directed toward the development of an action-research model which would assist other schools and communities faced with similar situations. The elements of the model are summarized below. While the inclusion of all the elements may not be a necessary condition for an effective action-research program, it is recommended that programs in which all the elements are present receive the highest priority.

Elements in the Action Phase

Triangulated Support

Three elements--administrative support, community action, and technical assistance--were present and cooperating. The project had the backing of top administrative officials. Leaders from the community were mounting community action programs and insisting that the school respond to the needs of the minorities. Technical assistance for an effective response was available on a reciprocal basis (the district provided a base of research and the researcher, his technical assistance).

Adequate Lead Time

Two and one-half months during the summer were used to prepare the infrastructure for the training program. Decisions regarding the scope and sequence of the program were made before the teachers started work in the autumn. This permitted recruitment of teachers before they had committed themselves to other activities.

Volunteer Enrollment

Only teachers who volunteered for the course actually participated. None were required to attend by the district. All participants paid a registration fee.

Extended Duration

The duration of the course over ten weeks allowed time for new ideas to sink in and for changes to take place. The participants were not dealt with in a superficial manner as is usually the case with one-day in-service programs; nor were they overloaded with new material, which might have happened if the course had been compressed into a one-week intensive program with a three-hour meeting each day.

Authentic Presentations of Information

The speakers were for the most part representatives of the cultural group in which the teachers were interested. The teachers were brought face-to-face with men they might not have otherwise met or conversed with. This exposure provided a real-life atmosphere, which would not have been present had the speakers been knowledgeable about the culture but not representative of it.

Incentives to Participate

Teachers being the busy people they are, it was necessary to provide them with incentives to participate in the training program. University credit and financial assistance were important incentives. In addition, the course was perceived as being relevant to the needs of the teachers and problems they faced in the classroom.

Small-Group Discussions

Each of the presentations of information was followed by small-group discussions led by a qualified discussion leader. In the discussions, teachers were able to exchange views relating to the topics presented each evening and also to integrate the information provided over the ten weeks.

Opportunities for Fieldwork

The course was planned to prepare the teachers for making home visits and to support them during the trial period of initial home visiting. Although home visits were not a requirement of the course, a deliberate effort was made to motivate teachers to visit homes by building up their self-confidence in communicating across cultural barriers. The fieldwork provided the teacher with an opportunity for going beyond her usual routine and thereby assisted her in doing something she might not otherwise have done.

Elements in the Research Component

Research Design

The design employed was a pretest-posttest control group design with replication. Participants were randomly placed in two training groups. One group received training in the autumn quarter, the other group, in the winter quarter. The winter group thus served as a control for the autumn group. The second training program provided the opportunity for replication.

Data Collection Instrument

The data collection instrument was a questionnaire developed by Harold Jonsson and modified for use with teachers of Mexican-American children. Four distinguishable subscales were identified for each of two major attitudinal dimensions--tolerance and optimism. One subscale was selected from each dimension for purposes of testing the research hypotheses. Information used to determine the validity of the subscales was gathered through structured classroom observations and teacher interviews, in addition to interviews with principals and students.

Benefits and Costs of the Action-Research Model

Several benefits accrued as a result of the particular research design employed. The fact that a treatment group and a comparison group were used meant that greater definition could be given the results than if only a treatment group had been used. By giving the comparison group the replication treatment, both groups eventually received training. Moreover, the replication allowed for testing modifications and improvements in the program format.

The principal costs involved were the elements of risk which attend any field experiment. There was uncertainty about the availability of suitable numbers of participants, the continued support from the administration, and the continued encouragement from community leaders. There was a risk of losing significant numbers of participants once they had enrolled. There were also temporal factors which could not be controlled for. Costs such as the ones mentioned no doubt account for the paucity of similar research studies.

In spite of the costs, it is recommended that the design employed in this research become standard in field experiment and in-service training situations, in which a research capability can be built into the training program. The benefits to the district are unquestionable, and through practice, improved designs will be developed which will permit minimization of risk borne by the researcher.

RESULTS OF THE ANALYSIS

An analysis of pretest scores revealed no significant differences among teachers along the tolerance dimension. In terms of the typology, the medians of all the teacher subgroups were located in the region described as "moderate."

In optimism dimension scores, teachers with one to six years of experience in the district who had over one year of experience with disadvantaged children were significantly higher than beginning teachers or those with seven or more years of experience. The median score of the highly optimistic subgroup was in the area described as "idealistic."

The first training program affected teacher tolerance in an opposite direction than did exposure to the status quo. Teachers exposed to the training program became more liberal in orientation, while those in the comparison group became more conservative.

The first training program also increased teacher optimism. Teachers exposed to the training program became more idealistic. Those in the comparison group did not change significantly.

Changes in the tolerance dimension were replicated by the second training program. Changes in the optimism dimension were not.

It appears that contact with children in the classroom may be sufficient to increase teacher optimism about pupil achievement potential. The evidence suggests that teachers with some experience have greater optimism than teachers with no experience or teachers with considerable years of experience. Increased experience and exposure do not have a predictable effect on optimism. What exposure to members of the group does affect is tolerance, by increasing the extent to which the teacher is able to identify with the problems of the disadvantaged learner. This increased empathy together with a greater understanding of ways in which the school system acts to remove the child from his culture increases the teacher's propensity to change her approach and to have changes introduced in the school system, in the form of greater experimentation and more deliberate attempts to harness the potential contribution of the Mexican-American children to the classroom.

POLICY RECOMMENDATION

As a result of the analysis, it is possible to make a policy recommendation for districts where significant numbers of minority children are enrolled. Implementation of this policy would lend itself to improved teaching-learning effectiveness in the classrooms.

In districts where there are no provisions for in-service training of new teachers, new teachers with less than a year of experience with disadvantaged children should not be placed in classroom situations where there is a large percentage of disadvantaged children. The best fit would be with teachers who have had some experience in the district and at least a year's experience with disadvantaged children, since these teachers would be most optimistic about such children's achievement potential.

In districts that can provide in-service training, programs such as the one described, having overall positive effects, should be widely adopted. The effect will be to produce teachers who are more liberal in their attitudes towards ethnic minorities and who have greater empathy for the Mexican-American than before the program.

APPENDIXES

APPENDIX

A

FORMATION AND TREATMENT OF TREATMENT AND MATCHED COMPARISON GROUPS

PROCEDURE FOR RANDOMIZED PLACEMENT IN TREATMENT AND CONTROL GROUPS

Once the approval of each participating district had been obtained, a tentative course outline and an application form were sent to each teacher through the official summer mailing to teachers from the District Offices. The total number of teachers thus contacted was approximately 1,200.

One hundred thirteen (approximately 11 percent) of those contacted returned application forms by the end of August. A pretest questionnaire was then mailed to each of the 113 with instructions to complete the questionnaire and return it before the commencement of school.

On the basis of the information contained in the application form, teachers were matched in pairs according to the following:

1. Specialization
2. Years of teaching experience
3. Work with disadvantaged children
4. Present teaching district.

Participants, by specialization, were divided into two categories: teachers, on the one hand, and administrators and specialists, on the other. Eight levels of experience were allowed for, and three levels of work with disadvantaged children.

Appendix Table 1 illustrates the matched pairs arrived at for teachers with no previous teaching experience. Teachers were separated from administrators and specialists and placed in eight groups according to years of teaching experience in the district, coded in the second and sixth columns.

Each teacher was assigned a three-digit number, the first digit of which was coded to represent one of the three districts. Half of the teachers in each experience level were selected at random and ranked in order of length of work with disadvantaged children, as shown in Appendix Table 1. The remainder of the teachers in that experience level were then matched as closely as possible with teachers in the first column by the rules outlined below:

1. Select a match for the first teacher in treatment group from the list of teachers in control group with the same level of work with disadvantaged children (hereafter called "exposure level"). If available, select a teacher from the same district.

2. If no match is available from the same district, proceed to the next exposure level and select the next unmatched teacher within that level.

3. If no match is available from the same district, select a teacher from another district with the same experience and exposure level.

4. If no match is available within the same exposure level, proceed to the next higher exposure level and attempt to match there before moving to the next higher experience level.

5. In all cases, matching should conform to the priorities outlined above.

Once the matched pairs were completed, random assignment to the first or second training program was performed with the help of a random numbers table. A beginning point was slected in the table, at random, and consecutive integers were used to determine whether a teacher would be placed in the first or second course. An even number was randomly decided to mean placement in the first course; an odd number would therefore mean placement in the second course. Referring to the illustrative Appendix Table 1, Teacher No. 110 was first on the list and the matched pair No. 106, was placed in the second, or winter course. The same procedure was followed until all teachers were placed in either the fall or winter course.

While the application forms were being coded and before the results of the course placement had been announced, all teachers who had expressed interest (113) were mailed the pretest questionnaire. Teachers were asked to return the questionnaire before the beginning of school, to ensure that the results would be free of influence by the first days of contact with the students. This precaution was particularly important in the case of new teachers.

APPENDIX TABLE 1

Illustration of Matched Pair Preparation for Random Placement in Training Course

(Number of Years of Experience in District)

Treatment Group				Control Group		
No. of Teacher	Experience in District	Contact	Pair	No. of Teacher	Experience in District	Contact
110	0	0	1	106	0	0
001	0	0	2	028	0	1
040	0	1	3	114	0	1
102	0	1	4	120	0	1
216	0	1	5	217	0	2
003	0	2	6	010	0	2

Shortly after the end of the first week of school, teachers were notified of the course in which they had been placed. Of the ninety-eight individuals who returned the pretest, fifty-one were placed in the fall course and forty-seven in the winter course. After being notified of the placement, sixteen teachers expressed the desire to switch courses. Switching was discouraged since it would make the groups less comparable due to self-selection. When teachers could not be talked out of switching, their wishes were followed. Not all those who expressed a desire to change did, in fact, change their placement. Of those who changed, ten asked to be changed from the autumn to the winter course, and six asked to be changed from the winter course to the fall course. Of those six, four actually joined the fall course, whereas only two of the ten requesting placement in the winter course actually attended that course. Of the total requesting a change of placement, ten (62 percent) did not register for the course in which they had asked to be placed. Eighty percent of those requesting a change from autumn to winter did not register for the winter course. Thirty-three percent of those requesting to be changed from winter to autumn did not register for the autumn course.

The membership of the two groups was further affected by the teachers who dropped out of the course before taking it. Fourteen of the fifty-one (27 percent) who had been expected in the first course did not sign up. Dropouts from the second course were even more numerous. Twenty-two of the forty-seven people (47 percent) who had been placed in the second course did not register.

Of the ninety-eight people who had expressed an interest in the course and who had completed the pretest, thirty-one registered for the autumn course, and twenty-one registered for the winter course. Four people who had been placed in the winter course took the autumn course, and two people who had been placed in the autumn course took the winter course.

Of those who took the first training program, twenty-eight returned usable posttests. Nineteen of those who were planning to take the second training program returned usable posttests, twenty-seven of those who had decided not to take either course returned usable posttests. (The preceding discussion is summarized in the flow chart, Appendix Figure 1.) Tables 2 and 3 summarize background information collected from the teachers. More detailed information (presented in Table 3) was collected from 33 teachers interviewed at the end of the second training program. The comparative data in Table 2 reveal the extent to which the sample of 33 was representative of the 98 who completed the pretest. The representative sample was used in the analysis presented in Appendix E.

(Text continues on page 85.)

APPENDIX FIGURE 1

Flow Chart: Numerical Summary of Participating Educators
(from initial contact through conclusion of posttest)

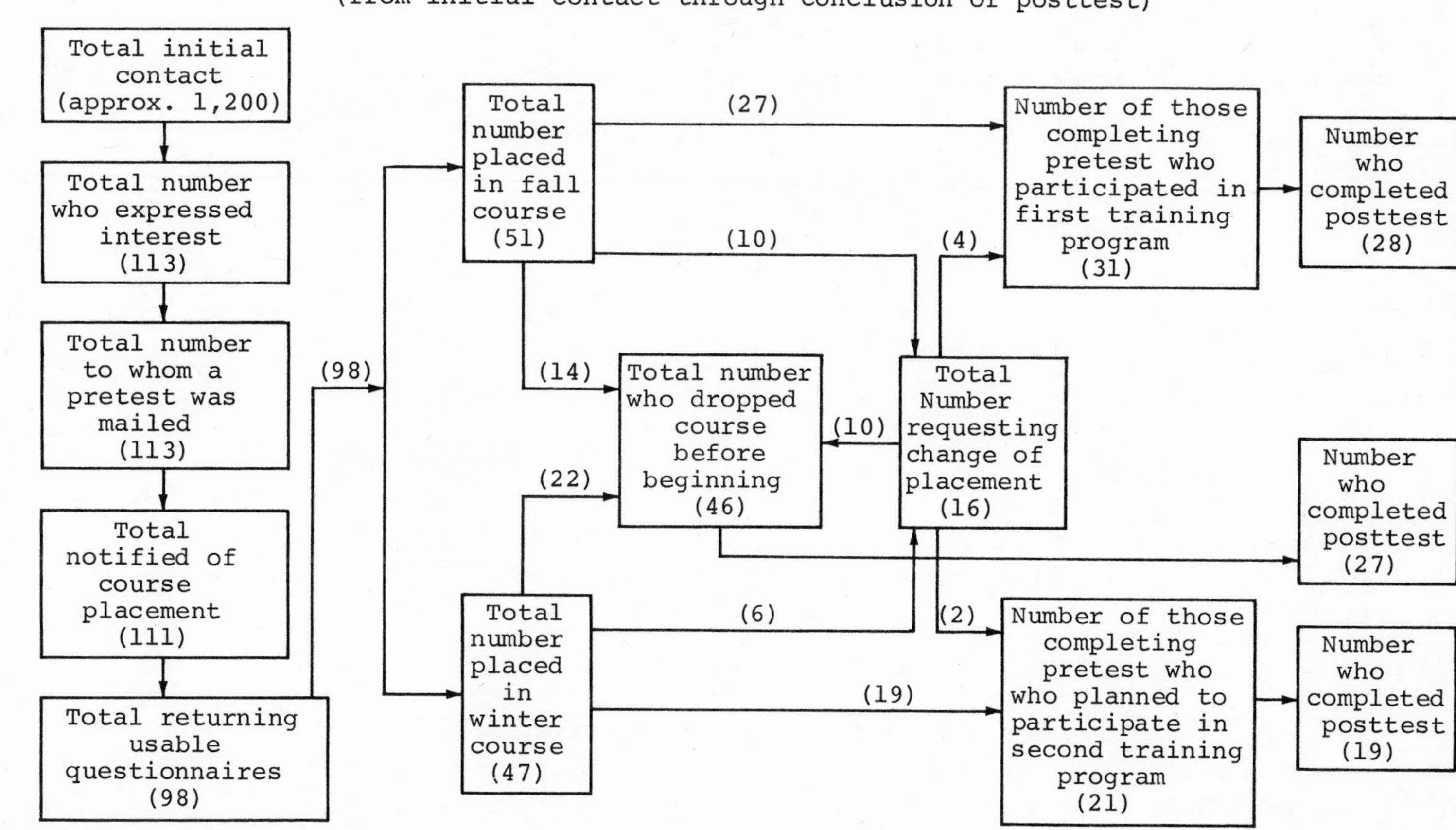

APPENDIX TABLE 2

Comparison of Representative Sample and Total Participants

Background Characteristic	Total Participants Completing Pretest (N=98)		Representative Sample (N=33)		Difference Between Sample and Total
	Number	Percent	Number	Percent	Percent
Sex					
Male	15	15.3	7	21.2	5.9
Female	83	84.7	26	78.8	-5.9
Size of District by Enrollment (K-8)					
10,358	31	31.6	7	21.2	-10.4
3,688	22	22.4	4	12.1	-10.3
2,654	45	45.9	22	66.7	20.8
Percentage of Mexican-American Children in Schools					
25-35	19	19.4	8	24.3	4.9
15-24	49	50.0	16	48.5	-1.5
0-14	30	30.6	9	27.3	-3.3
Grade					
7-8	11	11.6	5	15.2	3.6
5-6	15	15.8	6	18.2	2.4
3-4	23	24.2	7	21.2	-3.0
1-2	20	21.1	6	18.2	-2.9
Pre and K	7	7.4	3	9.1	1.7
Specialists and Administrators	19	20.0	6	18.2	-1.8

Background Characteristic	Total Participants Completing Pretest (N=98)		Representative Sample (N=33)		Difference Between Sample and Total
	Number	Percent	Number	Percent	Percent
Years of Teaching Experience					
7 or more	48	49.0	19	57.5	8.5
1-6	36	36.7	10	30.3	-6.4
None	14	14.3	4	12.1	-2.2
Years of Experience in District					
7 or more	30	30.6	11	33.4	2.8
1-6	42	42.9	16	48.5	5.6
None	26	26.5	6	18.2	-8.3
Experience with Disadvantaged					
Over 2 years	48	49.0	23	69.7	20.7
1-2 years	23	23.5	4	12.1	-11.4
Less than 1 year	27	27.6	6	18.2	-9.4
Knowledge of Spanish					
Some	57	58.2	22	66.7	8.5
None	41	41.8	11	33.3	-8.5
Participation in Course					
First Course	31	31.6	9	27.3	-4.3
Second Course	21	21.4	20	60.6	39.2
Dropped	46	46.9	4	12.1	-34.8

APPENDIX TABLE 3

Background Description of Teachers of Representative Sample*
(N = 33)

Characteristic	Number	Percent
Place of Birth		
California	11	33.3
Elsewhere	22	66.7
No. of Brothers and Sisters		
Seven-Eight	1	3.0
Five-Six	2	6.1
Three-Four	8	24.3
One-Two	20	60.6
Zero	2	6.1
Urban or Rural Background		
Urban	25	75.8
Rural	8	24.2
Status of Father's Occupation		
High	13	39.4
Middle	16	48.6
Low	4	12.1
Rank in Family		
First born	8	24.2
Second	12	36.4
Third	8	24.2
Fourth	4	12.1
Fifth	0	0.0
Sixth	1	3.0
Generation American		
First Generation	8	24.2
Second or More	25	75.8

Characteristic	Number	Percent
Years of Education Beyond High School		
Eight	1	3.0
Seven	3	9.1
Six	4	12.1
Five	15	45.5
Four	10	30.3
Age (Estimate)		
50-59	8	24.3
40-49	11	33.3
30-39	8	24.3
20-29	6	18.2
Similarity of Background to Mexican-American		
None	26	78.8
Some	7	21.2
Place of Training		
California	17	51.5
Elsewhere	16	48.5
Number of Children		
Four	6	18.2
Three	9	27.3
Two	5	15.2
One	4	12.1
Zero	9	27.3

*Teachers contacted on completion of second training program.

PROCEDURE FOR THE FORMATION OF TREATMENT AND MATCHED COMPARISON GROUPS FOR DATA ANALYSIS

For purposes of analysis, the decision was made to match the treatment group with teachers from the comparison group who were planning to take the second course and those who had decided not to take the course. Priority went to teachers planning to take the second course. They were matched first. Those remaining were used when there were no longer any available in the priority group. Since there were only nineteen in the priority group, nine teachers from the remainder were needed to complete the matching required for the analysis. A detailed description of the procedure employed appears below:

Treatment group individuals were matched to individuals in the comparison group according to the following criteria:

1. Years of teaching experience in the present district
2. District the teacher came from
3. Participation in the second course or in neither course
4. Pretest score
5. Experience with disadvantaged children, two or more years, or zero to one years. Only with new teachers was it possible to make this division.

Three-digit cases were formulated to describe and match participants. The <u>first</u> digit represented the categories of experience in teaching and working with disadvantaged children:

1 = 0 years' teaching experience and 0-1 years with disadvantaged children
2 = 0 years' teaching experience and 2+ years with disadvantaged children
3 = 1-6 years' teaching experience and 2+ years with disadvantaged children
4 = 7+ years' teaching experience and 2+ years with disadvantaged children.

The <u>second</u> digit represented the teacher's district. The <u>third</u> digit represented whether the teacher was

0 = in the first treatment group
1 = in the second treatment group
2 = in the group that did not receive training.

The first treatment group was identified by the letter "T", and the other two, comparison groups, were identified by the letter "C." (The arrangement of the cases is shown in Appendix Tables 4 and 5.)

The rules for matching were the following: beginning with group T-1-1-0, proceed in alphabetical order, matching each individual in that group with the individual in matching group C-1-1-1 who is closest in pretest tolerance and optimism scores.

If an individual in C-1-1-1 has been matched with more than one individual in T-1-1-0, then assign him to the closest match and find another individual in C-1-1-1 to match with the rejected T-1-1-0 individual(s). If C-1-1-1 is exhausted, then turn to C-1-1-2 for the match. Match each of the individuals with the available individuals who are from the same district before cross-matching any T individual with a C individual from another district. After T-1, T-2, and T-3 have been matched with all available individuals in their respective C groups, then find the best match for the remaining T individuals with the remaining unmatched C individuals within the category.

In the case of a tie, when two T individuals are equally matched with C individual, randomly determine the match.

(Text continues on page 89.)

APPENDIX TABLE 4

Total Cases Available for Matching by Tolerance and Optimum Scores

Years of Experience in Present District																	
New (0)						Intermediate (1-6)						Experienced (7+)					
Treatment			Control			Treatment			Control			Treatment			Control		
No.	Tol.	Opt.	No.	Tol.	Opt.	No.	Tol.	Opt.	No.	Tol.	Opt.	No.	Tol.	Opt.	No.	Tol.	Opt.
T-1-1-0			C-1-1-1			T-3-1-0			C-3-1-1			T-4-1-0			C-4-1-1		
047	11	17				011	12	25	002	16	24	004	11	20	009	11	19
			1-1-2			014	15	17	024	11	20	005	10	22	015	15	20
			001	14	26	019	20	28	025	13	25	008	16	21	035	10	18
			040	15	29	020	11	25	027	15	14	016	12	22			
			048	15	24	022	14	22	039	10	22	021	13	20	4-1-2		
						026	14	17				038	15	20	042	14	17
1-2-0			1-2-1			036	08	25	3-1-2						043	15	20
110	08	23	120	15	16	044	10	20	012	11	26						
						049	14	18	018	18	22	4-2-0			4-2-1		
			1-2-2						031	14	23	118	13	22	111	06	26
			102	12	21							124	15	20	130	10	17
			106	13	18	3-2-0			3-2-1								
									109	11	23				4-2-2		
1-3-0			1-3-2						116	15	17				117	09	21
206	12	19	216	11	23				123	11	24				121	14	21
									131	13	23						
												4-3-0			4-3-1		
T-2-1-0			C-2-1-1						3-2-2			224	14	22	213	11	21
017	13	21	010	16	23				101	09	22						
032	14	19							102	13	25				4-3-2		
037	13	22	2-1-2						125	09	20				203	15	21
															208	15	17
2-2-0			2-2-1			3-3-0			3-3-1						211	14	17
113	12	20				209	11	23	204	09	22				220	14	23
			2-2-2			218	11	19	228	14	22						
			108	16	27	226	09	23									
			122	14	22				3-3-2								
			129	10	18				212	15	24						
									223	14	18						
			2-3-1														
			217	13	22												
			2-3-2														
			215	12	23												

APPENDIX TABLE 5

Matched Individuals

Years of Experience in Present District																	
New (0)						Intermediate (1-6)						Experienced (7+)					
Treatment			Control			Treatment			Control			Treatment			Control		
No.	Tol.	Opt.	No.	Tol.	Opt.	No.	Tol.	Opt.	No.	Tol.	Opt.	No.	Tol.	Opt.	No.	Tol.	Opt.
047	11	17	048	15	24	011	12	25	025	13	25	004	11	20	009	11	19
	12	24		16	22		13	24		11	26		10	21		09	22
110	08	23	120	15	16	014	15	17	027	15	14	005	10	22	035	10	18
	10	22		10	17		15	23		17	17		07	26		06	18
206	12	19	216	11	23	019	20	28	018	18	22	008	16	21	043	15	20
	12	19		11	23		17	26		14	21		14	22		15	18
						020	11	25	039	10	22	016	12	22	203	15	21
							10	21		11	23		13	25		13	20
017	13	21	217	13	22	022	14	22	002	16	24	021	13	20	042	14	17
	14	20		12	17		15	22		13	27		12	23		11	21
032	14	19	106	13	18	026	14	17	212	15	24	038	15	20	015	15	20
	14	19		11	23		17	17		13	22		13	18		15	19
037	13	22	010	16	23	036	08	25	012	11	26	118	13	22	111	06	26
	14	23		14	26		10	23		13	29		14	22		08	22
113	12	20	122	14	22	044	10	20	024	11	20	124	15	20	130	10	17
	13	19		14	21		11	17		09	19		12	23		09	18
						049	14	18	031	14	23	224	14	22	213	11	21
							14	19		14	23		14	22		13	20
						209	11	23	228	14	22						
							11	24		14	24						
						218	11	19	223	14	18						
							13	21		14	17						
						226	09	23	204	09	23						
							10	22		09	19						

PROCEDURE TO TEST TEACHERS' PERCEIVED SIMILARITY TO MEXICAN-AMERICANS

The research design called for a situation in which the teachers would perceive their own background as being dissimilar to that of their Mexican-American students. Accordingly, teachers were provided in the course evaluation form with the following question, which was intended to test the closeness of fit of the setting to the design:

How similar is your background to that of your Mexican-American students?

1 2 3 4 5 6 7
Low similarity High similarity

(The responses to this item are shown in Appendix Table 6.)

APPENDIX TABLE 6

Distribution of Teachers on the Perceived Similarity of Background Scale Reported for Both Groups After the Training Program
(N = 72)

		Perceived Similarity Scale						
Group*	Frequency	Low 1	2	3	4	5	6	High 7
T	Absolute	18	11	5	5	5	2	0
	Relative	39.1	23.9	10.9	10.9	10.9	4.3	0.0
C	Absolute	4	10	3	5	2	2	0
	Relative	15.4	38.5	11.5	19.2	7.7	7.7	0.0
Total	Absolute	22	21	8	10	7	4	0
	Relative	30.5	29.2	11.1	13.9	9.8	5.5	0.0

*Includes participants who completed the evaluation form but not the questionnaire.

The validity of the perceived similarity of background scale is supported by the fact that the three

Mexican-American discussion leaders rated themselves 6 or 7 on the scale. None of the teachers taking the course gave himself a 7 rating. Only 5.5 percent of the total group perceived themselves as similar enough to warrant a 6 on the scale, while 59.7 percent of the total number of respondents perceived their own backgrounds as being low enough in similarity to warrant a 1 or 2 on the perceived similarity scale.

The second training group appears to have been somewhat higher in perceived similarity than the first training group. The mean scale score of the second training group was 2.9, while the mean score of the first training group was 2.4. This may be a reflection of the self-selection factor, the teachers feeling most apprehensive or feeling least similar to the Mexican-Americans being represented to a greater degree in the first training program.

The data presented in Appendix Table 6 bear out the assumption that the site chosen for the research was appropriate for the research design.

APPENDIX B

TEACHING THE DISADVANTAGED: AN OPINION SURVEY

INSTRUCTIONS

The following questionnaire is intended to probe the opinions of teachers and prospective teachers toward teaching disadvantaged pupils. The latter are defined as pupils from the lowest socio-economic levels, a large proportion of whom are of ethnic minority groups. Throughout the questionnaire, the words "child" and "pupil" refer to children who are within the normal range physically and mentally, i.e., who do not meet the criteria for placement in classes for the physically handicapped or the mentally retarded. The word "normal," intended in this sense, is occasionally used as a reminder of this definition.

Some items might be answered differently if you are thinking of Negro children than if you are considering Mexican-Americans. When in doubt, read "Mexican-Americans raised in poverty."

Most important, please take the items at face value and give the most appropriate responses based on your experience and expectations. The items are not intended to be subtle or to assess your personality. The results will be known only to the investigator, will be released only in summary form for groups of respondents, and will be used only for continued study of teacher attitudes pertaining to disadvantaged children. Your responses will in no way affect decisions about you, academically, professionally, or otherwise.

Each item is to be judged according to one of the following categories: (a) Strongly agree, (b) Agree, (c) Disagree, and (d) Strongly disagree.

Your answers are to be indicated on the answer sheet by marking a heavy X on the appropriate "bubble." Please do not make extraneous marks on the answer sheet as they will cause difficulty in scoring. Space is provided on the answer sheet for entering your name, date, district, school, and phone number.

All the answers are to be entered on one answer sheet. Notice Part 1 and Part 2 of the answer sheet to correspond to Part 1 and Part 2 of the questionnaire. One sample answer has been done to demonstrate the proper method of marking.

Since the response categories do not include a "don't know" alternative, many respondents will have to make some difficult choices. If you are uncertain about the facts pertaining to an item, please select the response representing your best estimate as to what the facts are. The completeness of all questionnaire data is important to their utilization in further study.

PART 1

1. Disadvantaged family background places a "ceiling" on a child's achievement potential.
2. A teacher can design appropriate learning tasks for any normal child, regardless of his racial or socio-economic background.
3. Disadvantaged pupils especially need to know that you believe in them and their ability to learn.
4. If a child has consistently had unsuccessful learning experiences in the primary grades, it is practically impossible to motivate him to learn in the intermediate grades.
5. The fear aroused in some whites by civil rights demands is harmful to progress toward social justice.
6. In working with disadvantaged children, teachers should beware of placing too much emphasis on the children's emotional needs and not enough on achievement.
7. At the present time, Mexican-Americans need to learn to ask as much as the greater community is willing to give, and not more.
8. Even if family and neighborhood influences are highly unfavorable, it is possible for a good teacher, under favorable learning conditions, to "reach" virtually every normal child.
9. It is imperative for Mexican-Americans from ghetto-like areas to develop a sense of racial pride if they are to overcome feelings of inadequacy.

10. Any child who is physically and emotionally normal is able to learn academically under good classroom conditions.

11. Mexican-American militancy causes an acceleration of progress toward social justice.

12. Most children can be effectively motivated to learn without the teacher's becoming emotionally involved with them.

13. Most of the improvements in the status of Mexican-Americans must be brought about through the efforts of socially concerned whites.

14. Disadvantaged children especially need to feel accepted, even loved, by their teacher if they are to make optimal growth in the classroom setting.

15. In the classroom, Mexican-American children need to learn the behavioral standards more characteristic of the white majority.

16. Under favorable classroom circumstances, all normal children can learn to enjoy school learning.

17. There is a danger that pupils will exploit the teacher's desire to maintain friendly relationships with the children.

18. It is true that disadvantaged people, when they become more aware of their situations, tend to begin making unrealistic and disproportionate demands.

19. A child will respond well only to a teacher who is like the sort of adult the child hopes to become.

20. In the long run, humility and cooperativeness will serve the disadvantaged person better than aggressiveness and bravado.

21. If an otherwise normal child appears to be a nonachiever, it is at least partly the fault of the school.

22. Singling out the contributions to American culture made by Mexican-Americans is hypocritical and misleading.

23. Schools can provide effective incentives for learning to all normal children.

24. If a teacher accepts all children alike, regardless of how they perform, they will not do their best work.

25. Mexican-American children must learn that their own well-being depends on being able to get along with whites.

26. In the interests of social equality, emphasis on "pride in race" is undesirable.

27. It is crucial to make disadvantaged pupils realize that your efforts are on their behalf and that learning is to their advantage.

28. It is unrealistic for a teacher to expect to "reach" all of the pupils in a given class.

29. Few children are permanently failure-prone due to prior experience and background.

30. Schools have a unique and major responsibility in bringing about social change.

31. It is unrealistic for a minority group to expect to attain economic and political equality in this society while preserving the attributes of a distinct subculture.

32. Disadvantaged minority children are quick to suspect that they are being patronized when white authority figures are friendly and supportive.

33. Teachers have to give up on chronic non-achievers in order to devote instructional time to pupils who will profit by it.

34. Some children lack the basic, innate drives necessary to achieve in school.

35. Without major changes in other institutions and patterns of society, schools can do little to remedy the handicaps of disadvantaged children.

36. Teachers of disadvantaged minority children should not place a great deal of emphasis on developing manners and attitudes acceptable to the middle class.

37. If a child is persistently unresponsive to his teacher's efforts to involve him in learning tasks, there is little justification for the teacher to continue devoting valuable instructional time to him.

38. Teachers should not foster in Mexican-American children a tendency to differentiate the Mexican-American subculture from the greater community.

39. In general, disadvantaged children will learn better when the teacher maintains a somewhat impersonal attitude.

40. As disadvantaged pupils learn skills in communication and other behavioral areas, they should be encouraged to view them as alternatives, rather than replacements, for the ways of their own subculture.

41. The subculture of the Mexican-American has positive aspects that can enrich the experience of Anglo children.

42. If teaching conditions are good and the teacher has relatively full information about each pupil, the teacher can find ways of individualizing the curriculum that will promote achievement growth in any normal child, regardless of his socio-economic background.

43. The school and teacher cannot successfully compete with family and peers in the molding of a child's aspirations.

44. Schools cannot expect to provide a good education to children of low native ability.
45. It is irresponsible for a teacher to encourage minority children to believe that their ways are acceptable (i.e., to the middle class) if, in fact, they are not.
46. In our time, very few Mexican-Americans will attain a middle-class level of economic well-being without publicly conforming to white middle-class standards.
47. Teachers of disadvantaged pupils should convey the attitude that use of demonstrations and boycotts is constructive and justifiable in the interests of improved life conditions for disadvantaged groups.
48. A certain degree of assertiveness related to racial pride should be encouraged in minority children.
49. If learning is to take place, the child's nonschool environment must at least have furnished him with latent incentives.
50. It is pointless to encourage minority children to take pride in aspects of their subculture which are not acceptable in the majority.
51. In teaching disadvantaged children it is especially important to convey to them that your feelings are warm and genuine.
52. "Playing-up" minority children's pride in the "heritage" of their subculture is only a temporary device to win their confidence.
53. In the short run at least, Mexican-Americans need to be aware that they have to achieve better than Anglos in order to attain comparable social and economic well-being.

PART 2

1. A good affective relationship with the teacher, and a pleasant classroom atmosphere are crucial to the achievement growth of disadvantaged children.
2. Even children with superior native ability can be so damaged by early environmental influences that they become virtually unteachable.
3. A minority must conform to majority standards in order to achieve equal social and economic rewards.
4. Ability to progress from the concrete to the abstract in learning activities is primarily inherited.
5. A child's preschool environment and experiences largely determine the later limits of his school achievement.

6. Respect for intergroup differences should not lead to deemphasizing the need to conform to majority standards.

7. "Acceptance" of lower-class minority pupils probably involves several stages, according to the age of the children, but the ultimate goals should be the replacement of their initial mores and attitudes with more viable and widely accepted ones.

8. A teacher with a middle-class background is permanently handicapped in trying to understand and teach slum children.

9. Disadvantaged children of minority groups must come to look upon themselves as "making it on their own" without patronage by whites.

10. It is possible to construct a school environment which successfully combats the undesirable influences of home and peers and alters a child's self-view and aspirations.

11. A teacher should take care, in dealing with lower-class Mexican-American children, not to encourage dependency and submissiveness, however convenient these traits are in the classroom setting.

12. White teachers who act appreciative of aspects of "ghetto" culture are likely to be viewed as hypocritical or insincere by the children raised in that culture.

13. Class management techniques, especially with disadvantaged pupils, should mobilize the children's pride and initiative, rather than stress docility and cooperating-with-teacher.

14. The Mexican-American child who cooperates and achieves well is very likely to be seen as an obnoxious "teacher's pet" to his peers.

15. In dealing with disadvantaged children, teachers should avoid "breaking their spirit" in order to produce conformity but should try to adapt the learning situation to the population of the class.

16. If a teacher's minority pupils frequently suspect him of racial prejudice, they are probably correct.

17. In working with disadvantaged pupils, a teacher needs to view pupil behavior with minimum reference to middle-class morality, ethics, and etiquette.

18. Even if Mexican-American militancy is a misguided concept or ideology, it has at least temporary utility in the fight for social justice.

19. Assuming that all other curricular and situational matters were ideal, the teacher's personality would not be a very important factor in pupil achievement.

20. If Mexican-American and other minority children are to learn to play roles in adult life which are productive and personally satisfying, their classes should provide a racially balanced social microcosm permitting the development of social attitudes which are realistic, but favorable.

21. In a class with a large proportion of educationally disadvantaged children, repressive techniques of class management are unavoidable.

22. Whether a child achieves his full intellectual potential depends primarily on his relationships and experiences outside of school.

23. One of the main values of school integration is that Mexican-American and other minority children have opportunities to earn the esteem of white children at an age early enough to affect basic attitudes toward self and others.

24. Teachers should not encourage the tendency of many minority children to feel that they have to be "extra nice" in order to get along with children of other groups.

25. More than middle-class children, disadvantaged children need to understand (and help formulate) class rules and procedures, so that they do not learn conformity for its own sake.

26. If children do not consistently achieve in school learning, it is usually because insufficient effort is made to harness their interests and utilize their existing goals and aspirations.

27. If disadvantaged groups, especially as defined by ethnic or racial criteria, are to improve their lot as a whole, they must stand together and assert their demands as a group.

APPENDIX

C

CLASSROOM OBSERVATION RECORD

Teacher ________________________________ No. _____

Sex ______ Grade ______ Date ________ City _________

__________ School ___________________ Time _________

Observer ___________ No. of Pupils in Class ________

No. of Mexican-Americans __________

REMARKS

ACTIVITY OBSERVED
Teacher-directed _____
Independent _____
Group discussion _____
Multiple _____

PUPIL BEHAVIOR								
1. Withdrawn	1	2	3	4	5	6	7	Alert
2. Obstructive	1	2	3	4	5	6	7	Cooperative
3. Uncertain	1	2	3	4	5	6	7	Confident
4. Dependent	1	2	3	4	5	6	7	Self-directed

TEACHER BEHAVIOR								
5. Impatient	1	2	3	4	5	6	7	Understanding
6. Rigid	1	2	3	4	5	6	7	Flexible
7. Tense	1	2	3	4	5	6	7	Relaxed
8. Partial	1	2	3	4	5	6	7	Fair
9. Lock-step	1	2	3	4	5	6	7	Diversified
10. Temperamental	1	2	3	4	5	6	7	Steady

---

*Based on Ryans 1960.

11.	Cold	1	2	3	4	5	6	7	Warm
12.	Aloof	1	2	3	4	5	6	7	Involved
13.	Condescending	1	2	3	4	5	6	7	Respectful
14.	Impersonal	1	2	3	4	5	6	7	Personal
15.	Critical	1	2	3	4	5	6	7	Supportive
16.	Defensive	1	2	3	4	5	6	7	Open

PUPIL BEHAVIOR

1. Withdrawn--Alert

Withdrawn	Alert
1. Pays no attention	1. Actively follows teacher's directions
2. Sleepy, not participating	2. Eager to participate
3. Attention wanders	3. Concentrates

2. Obstructive--Cooperative

Obstructive	Cooperative
1. Causes commotion	1. Tries to please
2. Talks behind teacher's back	2. Speaks only when called on
3. Throws things	3. Orderly
4. Wanders around room	4. Stays in seat
5. Bothers others	5. Minds own business
6. Repeatedly asks questions	6. Listens the first time
7. Acts fresh with teacher	7. Polite
8. Unprepared	8. Prepared

3. Uncertain--Confident

Uncertain	Confident
1. Hesitant	1. Wants to be first
2. Gets clues from others	2. Does his own work
3. Nervous (e.g., nail-biting)	3. Relaxed and unafraid

4. Dependent--Self-directed

Dependent	Self-directed
1. Needs to be told what to do	1. Sees what needs to be done
2. Cannot work long on his own	2. Can work by himself for long periods
3. Unable to respond when called on--needs prompting	3. Has answer ready when called on--responds without prompting
4. Unwilling to assume responsibility	4. Eager to take the lead

TEACHER BEHAVIOR

5. Impatient--Understanding

Impatient	Understanding
1. Harps at kids "How many times do I have to tell you . . ."	1. Listens, waits

2. Threatens kids	2. Explains why it is necessary
3. Sends students out of room	3. Puts up even with rowdiest
4. Shows no understanding of background factors	4. Understands and takes into account, e.g., allows time in school for completion of homework
5. Ridicules children	5. Protects children from ridicule

6. Rigid--Flexible

1. Insists on a single standard of academic work	1. Adapts goals to individual needs

7. Tense--Relaxed

1. Doesn't let the kids get away with anything	1. Casts a blind eye to certain forms of behavior (types of aggressive behavior towards teacher)
2. Makes every incident an occasion for a lecture	2. Smooths over potentially critical incidents
3. Insists on punctuality and attendance (makes a scene if someone is late)	3. Not upset by latecomers
4. Expects conformance to a single norm (determined by teacher)	4. Accepts variations in student behavior without judging
5. On guard against interruptions	5. Not bothered by interruptions

8. Partial--Fair

1. Shows favoritism	1. Applies same rules to all
2. Rules not expressly stated	2. Rules explicit
3. Always calls on same students	3. Calls on different students
4. Gives some students special advantages	4. Gives everyone a chance
5. In case of controversy, listens to only one side	5. In case of controversy, listens to both sides of the story

9. Lock-step--Diversified

Lock-step	Diversified
1. Seldom gives individual attention	1. Frequently gives attention on individualized activities
2. Spends much time lecturing	2. Spends much time talking to individuals or small groups
3. Everyone does same things at same time	3. Many activities permitted simultaneously

10. Temperamental--Steady

Temperamental	Steady
1. Erratic	1. Steady
2. Blows her stack	2. Keeps her lid on
3. Shows her temper	3. No outward sign of temper
4. Inconsistent	4. Predictable
5. Makes empty threats	5. Follows through

11. Cold--Warm

Cold	Warm
1. Straight face--very serious looking	1. Smiling face--happy looking
2. Blunt, to the point	2. Talkative
3. Does not appear to listen and does not seem interested in the person	3. Appears to listen attentively and shows an interest in the person

12. Aloof--Involved

Aloof	Involved
1. Minds own business	1. Knows about the activities of students
2. Hard to reach	2. Works in with kids
3. Seldom touches children	3. Often touches children
4. Stiff and formal	4. Approachable to all students

13. Condescending--Respectful

Condescending	Respectful
1. Puts students down	1. Builds students up
2. Impressed with own importance	2. Impresses students with their importance
3. Talks down to students	3. Talks to students as deserving respect

14. Impersonal--Personal (Associatedness)

1. Does not become involved with student problems	1. Is involved with student problems and takes personal interest in helping the student who is in difficulty
2. "Professional"	2. Associates with children outside school
3. Expects parents to come to school	3. Makes home visits

15. Critical--Supportive

1. Finds fault	1. Draws attention to positive things
2. Unpleasant--can't be bothered	2. Interested--always has time

16. Defensive--Open

1. Withholds information from observer	1. Volunteers information to observer
2. Supersensitive to criticism	2. Asks for criticism and accepts it

APPENDIX D

A CYBERNETIC MODEL OF THE EDUCATIONAL PROCESS

FORMULATION OF THE MODEL

The conceptual framework used to explore unmeasured effects of the training program is a cybernetic model of the educational process, developed during the research. In what follows, each element of the model (illustrated in Appendix Figure 2) is described in theoretical terms.*

1. Student behavior constitutes the problem to be dealt with through the educational process. This dimension describes "what exists," or "what is," i.e., the situation to be changed or maintained.
2. Goals are the desired end-states or desired performance levels of student behavior. Goals state what ought to be. They may be thought of as desired directions of student growth.
3. Teaching procedures are the methods used to move student behavior in the normative direction.
4. Hypotheses are the conditional statements which link what the teacher does to the avowed goals. Hypotheses are of two sorts: background hypotheses or assumptions about the attributes a student brings to the classroom and procedural hypotheses, which are the assumptions the teacher makes about the methods to use with given students, to help the students grow in the desired direction, given their backgrounds.

---

*Important stimuli for the thinking that has gone into the development of this model have been the work of A. P. Coladarci (1967) and of E. F. Haskell and Harold Cassidy (1969), shared with the author by Cassidy in conversations before the publication of his book.

APPENDIX FIGURE 2

Cybernetic Model of the Educational Process

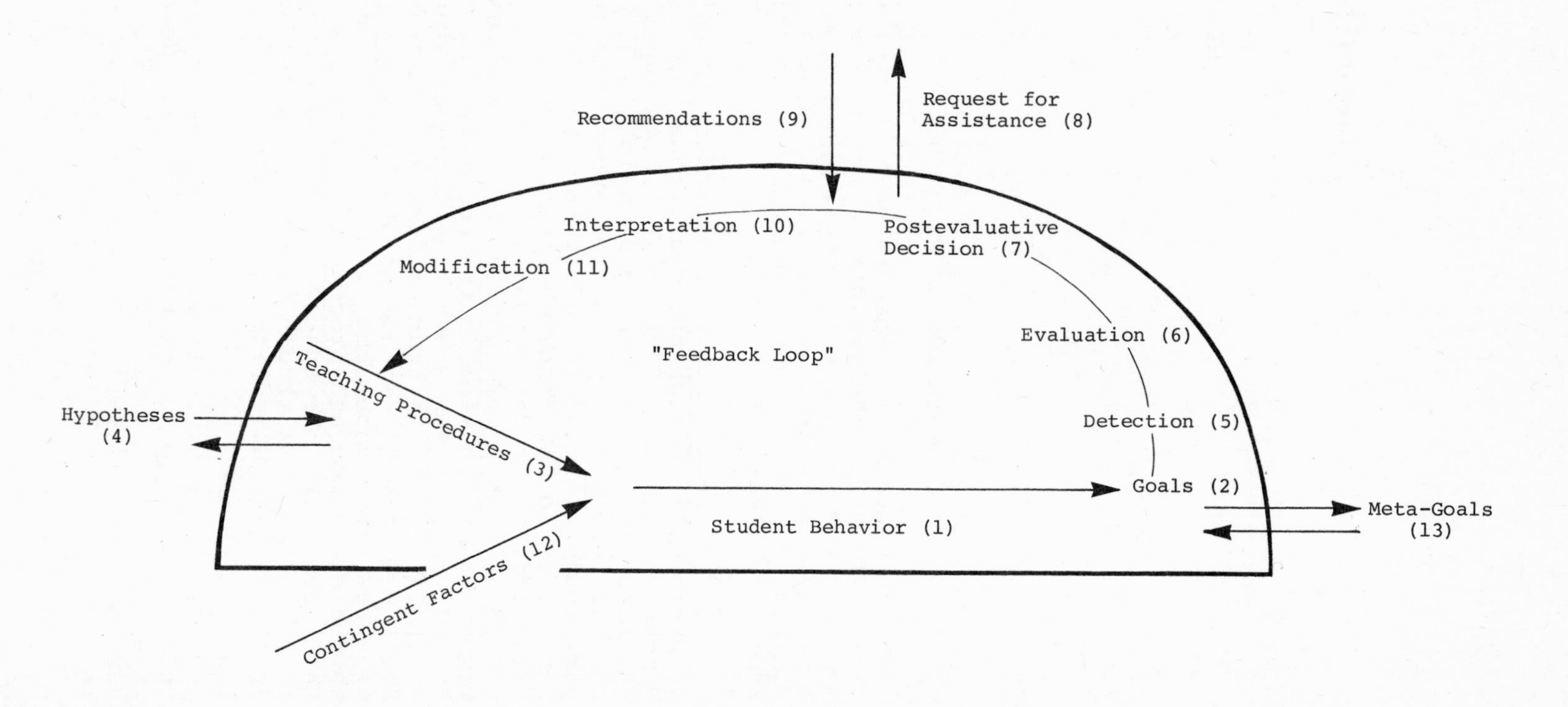

The feedback loop is constructed from several elements beginning with:

5. the instruments used for detection of students' progress.
6. Evaluation is dependent on the techniques used to monitor progress. Evaluation or error detection may be described by the following formula:

$$E = G - D,$$

where D = student behavior, detected through selected instruments,
E = error factor,
G = goals.

There are three possible outcomes:

1. E is greater than zero (normative exceeds actual behavior).
2. E is equal to zero (normative equals actual behavior).
3. E is less than zero (actual exceeds normative behavior).

In other words, the error factor (the extent to which goals and detected student behavior are not equal) may be positive, zero, or negative.

7. The postevaluative decision is what the teacher does after reorganizing the sign and size of E. In the first instance, in which goals exceed detected behavior, the teacher may decide to find new procedures, adjust the goals downward, or withdraw from the situation. In the second instance, the teacher has the options of finding less potent methods of increasing the goals to match the detected behavior.
8. A request for assistance will be made in the event that the teacher perceives the difference between goals and detected behavior to be larger than she is able to cope with, given her own resources.
9. Recommendations may touch on any of the elements in the model. The teacher may be advised to try new approaches or to lower her expectations to make the goals less removed from the actual behavior of the students.
10. Interpretation is a defense mechanism employed by the teacher. Advice rendered is interpreted on the basis of the teacher's knowledge of the classroom situation and her own tastes, preferences, and patterns of work. Interpretation constitutes

another step in the feedback process, in which new information is processed and judged relevant or not.

11. Modification is the end-point of the feedback loop. After information has returned to the teacher and passed through the teacher's defensive screens, it will be incorporated either as a new procedure or as an altered goal. Suggestions that are interpreted as relevant and feasible stand a better chance of being implemented by the teacher than suggestions which are not.

12. Contingent factors are the environmental influences that may hinder or help the process toward the desired end-states. These factors are usually beyond the control of the teacher but may have an overwhelming influence on the educational process.

13. Metagoals are superordinate or second-order goals that link what is done in the classroom to the larger institutional and societal setting. Metagoals include long-term objectives such as socialization, occupational readiness, or societal transformation.

OPEN-ENDED QUESTIONS FOR TEACHER INTERVIEWS BASED ON CYBERNETIC MODEL

1. How would you describe the range of behavior that you see in your Mexican-American children?

Academic

Interpersonal

2. What would you say are the goals you would like your children to reach?
3. How do you help the children reach those goals?
4. What would you say are some of the assumptions behind the way you work with your Mexican-American children? (I.e., what is your point of view regarding the Mexican-American and the larger society?)
5. What would you say are some of the main factors that influence the Mexican-American child's ability to reach those goals?

Expand on the way background factors influence behavior.

6. How do you check the student's progress?
7. How do you determine what a student's potential to achieve is?

How do you decide whether the child is working up to his potential?

How do you decide whether a child should be retained in grade?

8. To whom to you turn for help with your teaching?

What do you do if you have problems with your Mexican-American children?

9. Did you get any help from the course?
10. What suggestions have you been able to implement?
11. How have your attitudes toward the Mexican-American changed during the past year?

Please select the statement below that most closely describes your point of view.

A. Their out-of-school environment imposes serious limitations on what they can achieve in school, and the militant movement will do them more harm than good.

B. Their out-of-school environment does not seriously limit what they can achieve in school, and the militant movement is a positive way of bringing more attention to their situation.

C. Their out-of-school environment imposes serious limitations on what they can achieve in school, and the militant movement is a positive way of bringing more attention to their situation.

D. Their out-of-school environment does not impose serious limitations on what they can achieve in school, but militancy will do them more harm than good.

Please expand on the selection you made.

APPENDIX

E

ANALYSIS OF THE ASSOCIATION BETWEEN TEACHER BACKGROUND CHARACTERISTICS AND CHANGES IN SCORE

Although the following discussion goes beyond the intended scope of the study, it is included here for its potential contribution to the generation of further research. The sample of teachers who completed both pretest and posttest is representative in many ways but biased in others. (See comparisons with large sample in Table 2, Appendix A). Researchers interested in research on teacher characteristics might find several fruitful hypotheses by studying this appendix.

ASSOCIATION OF BACKGROUND VARIABLES WITH INITIAL ATTITUDE LEVELS

In an attempt to move beyond scale scores to a better understanding of the dynamics responsible for initial scores and changes, certain background data were collected from a representative sample of thirty-three teachers who had completed the pretest and the posttest. In what follows, we shall look first at the relationship between background variables and initial attitude levels. The next step will be to look at the relationship between background variables and the direction of change of both the tolerance and optimism scores.

Teacher background information included data about the district in which the teacher taught and the teacher's own personal background. It was supplied with returned pretests:

Size of the district

Percentage Mexican-American in the school
Percentage Mexican-American in the district
Grade level.

Of the variables of teacher background, four were supplied with returned pretests:

Sex
Total teaching experience
Experience teaching in the district
Experience with culturally different.

Other information about the teacher's background was collected at the end of the training program from a sample of thirty-three of the teachers who had taken the pretest. This sample included nineteen teachers who were randomly placed in the second training program, ten teachers who had taken the first course, and four teachers who had dropped the course. These variables included the following:

Experience with disadvantaged
Knowledge of Spanish
Marital status
Years of schooling beyond high school
Location of training
Number of children in own family
Age oldest child.

Finally, from biographical sketches completed by the teacher, additional information was collected:

Urban or rural background
Generation American
Age (estimate)
Expression of perceived similarity of background to that of Mexican-Americans.

From the questionnaires used in the analysis, the dependent variables were arrived at. These consisted of:

Tolerance of militancy
Optimism about the effect of environment

(Text continues on page 118.)

APPENDIX TABLE 7

Kendall Correlation Coefficients[a]

Variable Labels[b]	032	033	034	035	040	041	002	007	008	009	011	012	031	036	037	038	039	042	043	003	006	005	017	021	013
032					.41				.20[.10]										.21[.08]						
033					.25				.40						.56		.27	.42	-.26		.26			-.30	-.31
034				.57											.30	.37	.32	.33		-.20					
035						-.29									.22	.33				-.18[.10]					
040									.24		.35							.35	.22						
041							-.29		-.20			-.22	-.34	.24	.26				-.22						
002								(-.22)		(-.15)			.24		-.39					(.11)	(-.22)				
007									(.71)	(.57)	(.40)														
008										(.60)	(.41)	(.15)	.36				.38	.49							
009											(.63)														
011																		.23	.20						
012																-.32				(.12)	(.16)	(.13)			
031																.30	.51	.43					-.26		
036																				.27	.23[.06]		-.31		
037																				-.51			.24	-.21[.08]	
038																	.40	.34	.22[.06]						
039																		.71	.24						-.35
042																							-.23		-.30
003																					(.18)	(-.18)	(-.16)		
006																								(.16)	
005																								(.11)	
017																									(.26)
021																									(.62)

[a]Correlations are significant at .05 or better unless otherwise noted in square brackets. Figures in parentheses refer to information gathered from application form (N = 98). Figures not in parentheses refer to information drawn from post-training descriptive autobiographies (N = 33).

[b]Variable labels and their codes listed:

Type F: Family Background
032 Father's occupation
033 Place of birth
034 Number of brothers and sisters
035 Rank among siblings
040 Background urban or rural
041 Generation American

Type P: Personal Background
002 Sex
007 Total teaching experience
008 Experience in district
009 Experience with culturally different
011 Experience with disadvantaged
012 Knowledge of Spanish
031 Marital status
036 Years of schooling beyond high school
037 Location of training
038 Number of children in own family
039 Age oldest child
042 Age (estimate)
043 Expression of similarity to Mexican-American background

Type I: Institutional Background
003 Size of district
006 Grade level
005 Percent Mexican-American in school
004 Percent Mexican-American in district

Type D: Dependent Variables
017 Tolerance of militancy
021 Optimism about reenvironment

APPENDIX TABLE 8

Cross-Correlations of Selected Type I and Type P Variables--
Kendall Correlation Coefficients[a]
(N = 98)

Variable Number[b]	Sex 002	Distr Size 002	% Mex-Am Distr 004	% Mex-Am School 005	Grade 006	Total Exp 007	Exp Distr 008	Exp Cult Diff 009	Exp Disadv 011	Knowl Span 012
002		.11	-.11		-.22	-.22		-.15		
003			-1.00	-.18	.18					.12
004				.18	-.18					-.12
005										.13
006										.16
007							.71	.57	.40	
008								.60	.41	.15
009									.63	
011										
012										

[a]Only coefficients significant at the .05 level or better are reported.

[b]See Appendix Table 7, Footnote b for labels.

APPENDIX TABLE 9

Cross-Correlations of Background Variables (Types P and I) and Two Dependent Variables*
(N = 33)

Variable Type Number	P Marital Status 031	F Father Occup 032	F Birth-place 033	F Sib-lings 034	F Sib Rank 035	P Years School 036	P Loc of Train 037	P Chil-dren 038	P Age Oldest 039	F Urban/ Rural 040	F Gener Am 041	P Age 042	P Sim to Mex-Am 043
P Sex 002	.24						-.39				-.29		
I Size of District 003				-.20 [.10]		.27	-.51						
I Grade 006			.26			.23 [.06]							
P Total Experience 007													
P Exp in District 003	.36	.20 [.10]	.40						.38	.24	-.20	.49	
P Exp Disadvantaged 011										.35		.23	.20 [.10]
P Knowledge Spanish 012								-.32			-.22 [.07]		
Quadrant Score 013			-.31						-.35			-.30	
D Tolerance 017	.26					-.31	.24					-.23 [.06]	
D Optimism 021			-.30				-.21 [.08]						

*The significance level of the coefficient is .05 or smaller unless otherwise noted in square brackets.

APPENDIX TABLE 10

Cross-Correlation of Type P and F Variables--Kendall Correlation Coefficients*
(N = 33)

Variable Number	Marital Status 031	Father Occup 032	Birth-place 033	Sib-lings 034	Sib Rank 035	Years School 036	Loc of Train 037	Chil-dren 038	Age Oldest 039	Urban/ Rural 040	Gener Am 041	Age 042	Sim to Mex-Am 043
031								.30	.51		-.34	.43	
032										.41			.21 [.08]
033							.56		.27	.25		.42	-.26
034					.57		.30	.37	.32			.33	
035							.22	.33			-.29		
036											.24		
037											.26		
038									.40			.34	.22 [.07]
039												.71	.24
040												.35	.22 [.06]
041													-.22 [.06]
042													
043													

*The significance level of the coefficient is .05 or smaller unless otherwise noted in square brackets.

ASSOCIATION OF BACKGROUND VARIABLES WITH TOLERANCE SCORES

The variables in Appendix Table 11 are ranked by relative strength of association with the tolerance score.

APPENDIX TABLE 11

Association of Variables with Pretest Tolerance Scores

Variable	Chi Square	Significance
Years of education	2.21	.14
District status	1.24	.27
Experience in the district	1.01	.31

Years of Education

The more years of education the teacher has had, the more likely it was for the teacher to score relatively low on the tolerance scale. The data on which this generalization is based are in Appendix Table 12. In the table, it is noted that the percentages of those scoring above the median on the tolerance scale are approximately reversed when the two groups are compared. Seventy percent of those having only four years of college scored in the upper half of the tolerance scale, while 65 percent of those having six or more years of education beyond high school scored in the lower half of the scale.

APPENDIX TABLE 12

Relationship Between Years of Schooling and Tolerance

Pretest Tolerance Score	Education No. of Teachers	
	Below Median	Above Median
Above Median	7	8
Below Median	3	15

Note: Corrected chi square = 2.2, with 1 degree of freedom. Significance = 0.1. Lamda (asymmetric) = 0.27 with tolerance score dependent. Kendall's tau B = 0.3. Significance = 0.004. Gamma = 0.6.

The data may be interpreted to mean that those who have had more than a college education are more conservative and less supportive of the militant movement than those with only a college education. They seem to have a greater vested interest in the status quo.*

District Status

On the pretest it was noted that there was a tendency for teachers in the lower status district to be more likely to score in the upper half of the tolerance scale than the lower half; while in the higher status districts, the tendency was reversed: Teachers were more likely to score in the lower half of the scale rather than the upper half. As shown in Appendix Table 13, 27 percent of the teachers from the higher status districts scored above the median on the tolerance scale, compared with 54 percent of the teachers from the lower status districts.

---

*When the sample was divided into two age groups, one including those under forty and the other including those over forty, those with more education were still found to be lower in tolerance. In other words, age did not seem to be the crucial factor.

APPENDIX TABLE 13

Relationship Between the District Status and Tolerance

Pretest Tolerance Score	Status of District	
	Lower	Higher
Above Median	12	3
Below Median	10	8

Note: Lamda (asymmetric) = 0.13, with tolerance score dependent. Kendall's tau B = -0.26. Significance = 0.02. Gamma = -0.5.

The data may be interpreted to reflect the greater urgency felt among teachers in the lower status district. Teachers in that district were closer to the difficulties Mexican-American children were facing (the lower status district had a greater percentage of Mexican-American students than the higher status district). They were more aware of the lack of relevance in the school curriculum than teachers in the higher status districts and consequently tended to show more support for the demands for change expressed by the militants than did the teachers from the higher status districts.

Experience in the District

There was a tendency for teachers with more than three years of experience in the district to be lower in tolerance than teachers with three or less years of experience in the district. As shown in Appendix Table 13, 31 percent of teachers with over three years of experience in the district scored above the median on the tolerance scale, compared with 55 percent of the teachers with three years or less experience in the district.

APPENDIX TABLE 14

Relationship Between Length of Experience in the District and Tolerance

Pretest Tolerance Score	Experience in District	
	Below Median	Above Median
Above Median	11	4
Below Median	9	9

Note: Corrected chi square = 1.0, with 1 degree of freedom. Significance = 0.31. Lamda (asymmetric) = 0.13 with tolerance score dependent. Kendall's tau B = 0.2. Significance = 0.03. Gamma = 0.47.

These figures could be accounted for by two factors. As teachers gain experience in the district, they may become adjusted to the way things are and feel less a need for change than they did when they began in the district. A second factor that might account for some of the difference is the tendency of teachers to leave the lower status district after several years of experience, which makes the two groups somewhat different. In other words, that those who scored above the median in the more experienced group were a lower percentage could be accounted for by socialization to the educational system or by the departure of teachers with more change-oriented views.

BACKGROUND FACTORS ASSOCIATED WITH THE OPTIMISM SCALE

Three variables found to be significantly correlated with the optimism variable are reported in Appendix Table 15 in order of their strength of association.

APPENDIX TABLE 15

Variables Significantly Correlated with Pretest Optimism Score

Variable	Chi Square	Significance
Grade (coded by magnitude of problem)	5.37	.02
Place of birth (coded as Californian or outsider)	1.46	.10
Experience in the district	2.05	.15

Grade

Through the course of our observations, it appeared that there were four stages in the elementary educational process that presented differing degrees of difficulty for teacher and student alike. The first stage included the preschool and kindergarten; the second stage included the first and second grades; the third stage spanned the grades between third and sixth; and the fourth stage included the seventh and eighth grades.

In stage one, before the pressure is on to learn how to read and write, the teacher's task is concentrated on helping the child enjoy being in school in the company of other children and with a variety of playthings. In stage two, the teacher's major task is to teach the children to read and to begin writing. In stage three, the teacher's task is mainly supervising the development of skills the child was supposed to have acquired in the first and second grade. In stage four, the teacher's task is to prepare the child for more advanced work in high school or for the world of work outside the school system.

The stages in which teachers with Mexican-American students seemed presented with the greatest problems were stages two and four. In stage two they had the task of teaching English both as a second language and as a first language. In stage four, the teacher had to cope with students who were becoming more socially aware, physically more powerful (hence potentially more threatening), and more conscious of their identity as members of a minority group.

During the preschool years the Mexican-American child poses less of a problem for the teacher (even though--or perhaps because--at that age the child may be reflecting more of the culture of the home). During stage three, the children have learned to fit in. They may have already been retained in a grade once by that time; hence, may have had more experience than the other students in the class. They have acquired the ability by that time to survive in the classroom by being "nice and quiet."

If the preceding observations dealing with the stages of socialization in the school system are correct, one would expect to find differences in teacher attitudes at the different stages. More particularly, one would hypothesize that at the stages in which the Mexican-American child manifested greatest difficulty, the teachers would have lower levels of optimism than they would have at the stages in which the Mexican-American child showed less difficulty with schoolwork. Accordingly, teachers were coded in two groups on the basis of the magnitude of the problem they faced in the classroom. Teachers at stages one and three were coded as being in minor problem situations, whereas teachers at stages two and four were coded as being in major problem situations. The results of this coding and the chi square analysis are shown in Appendix Table 16.

APPENDIX TABLE 16

Relationship Between Problems in Grades and Optimism

Pretest Optimism Score	Magnitude of Problem	
	Minor	Major
Above Median	13	6
Below Median	3	11

Note: Corrected chi square = 5.37. Significance = .02. Lamda (asymmetric) = 0.36 with optimism score dependent. Kendall's tau B = -.46. Significance = .0001. Gamma = -0.77.

The results in Appendix Table 16 show that 79 percent of the teachers scoring below the sample optimism median were in situations defined as major problem situations. Twenty-one percent of teachers scoring below the optimism median for the sample were in minor problem situations. Thirty-two percent of teachers above the optimism median were in major problem situations, compared with 68 percent above the median who were in minor problem situations.

The analysis allows us to hypothesize that teachers working in situations in which the problems of the Mexican-American student are greater tend to have less optimism, to be less idealistic and more realistic, than teachers working in situations in which the problems of the Mexican-American students are fewer.

Place of Birth

When the teacher's place of birth was coded to indicate whether or not the teacher was a native Californian, significant differences emerged between the two groups of teachers, as shown in Appendix Table 17. Teachers who were native Californians were more likely to be above the median in optimism than teachers who were born elsewhere. Eighty-two percent of the native Californians in our sample scored above the median in optimism, while 46 percent of those who were born outside the state scored above the median.

APPENDIX TABLE 17

Relationship Between Place of Birth and Optimism

Pretest Optimism Score	Place of Birth	
	California	Elsewhere
Above Median	9	10
Below Median	2	12

Note: Corrected chi square = 2.6, with 1 degree of freedom. Significance = 0.106. Lamda (asymmetric) = 0.14 with optimism score dependent. Kendall's tau B = 0.35. Significance = 0.002. Gamma = 0.69.

There are a number of possible explanations for this relationship, which have to be investigated through further research. It may be that the native Californians are more likely to be teaching in minor problem situations, which would help account for their optimism being higher than that of outsiders. In our data we found that 36 percent of the native-born were teaching in major problem situations, compared with 59 percent of those born elsewhere. Kendall's Tau B was .21, significant at the .03 level. We lack the data to determine whether the attitudes of outsiders compared with natives are higher or lower in optimism before they start teaching.

There is a possibility that outsiders are placed in situations where vacancies are more likely to occur, i.e., in problem situations--and it is exposure to problem situations that make teachers less optimistic, more realistic, than native Californians, who, in a sense, are protected from the major problem situations. This type of reasoning, only conjectural, does seem worth pursuing.

It could also be that outsiders hold more negative stereotypes of the Mexican-American than Californians, who have had more contact with them. Because of their greater familiarity with Mexican-Americans, natives consider their home background less a handicap than do teachers without knowledge of their background.

A similar relationship to the one observed when teachers were categorized according to birthplace held up when teachers were categorized according to place of training. The pattern was less distinct with the older age group than it was for the younger age group. (Gamma for the younger group was -.68, while Gamma for the older group was -.27.) (See Appendix Table 18.)

Seventy-one percent of those trained in California scored above the median on the optimism scale, while 44 percent of those trained outside California scored above the median.

APPENDIX TABLE 18

Relationship Between Place of Training and Optimism

Pretest Optimism Score	Where Trained	
	California	Elsewhere
Above Median	12	7
Below Median	5	9

Note: Lamda (asymmetric) = 0.143 with optimism score dependent. Kendall's tau B = 0.271. Significance = 0.013.

Experience in the District

When teachers were grouped by years of experience in the district, the group with less than median experience was somewhat higher in optimism than the group with greater than median experience in the district. Seventy percent of the teachers with less than median experience (three years in the district or less) scored above the median on the optimism scale, compared with 38 percent of the teachers with more than the median level of experience in the district, as shown in Appendix Table 19.

APPENDIX TABLE 19

Relationship Between Years of Experience in the District and Optimism

Pretest Optimism Score	Experience in District	
	Below Median	Above Median
Above Median	14	5
Below Median	6	8

Note: Corrected chi square = 2.0, with 1 degree of freedom. Significance = 0.152. Lamda (asymmetric) = 0.21 with optimism score dependent. Kendall's tau B = 0.31. Significance = 0.005. Gamma = 0.58.

The fact that teachers with more experience tended to score below the median in optimism may be a result of prolonged exposure to the problems, which would tend to reduce idealism and make teachers more realistic. It could also be that teachers who were high in optimism tended to remain in the district only a few years, which would decrease the number who would have scored above the median had they remained in the district. In other words, the difference in score could be a result of exposure to the problem or a result of there being two different groups of teachers, with more optimistic teachers having a greater representation in the group with less than the median years of experience in the district.

ANALYSIS OF THE CHANGE SCORES TO DETERMINE RELATIONSHIPS BETWEEN BACKGROUND VARIABLES AND DETECTED CHANGE

As shown in Appendix Table 20, the most frequent occurrence, when changes in the two scales are considered together, was for the teachers to decrease in optimism and increase in tolerance. Thirty-nine percent of the sample of thirty-three changed in this manner. The least frequent outcome was for teachers to decrease on both scales. Seventeen percent of the twenty-three teachers changed in a negative direction on both scales. Equal numbers of teachers (22 percent of the total) are shown to have increased on both scales or increased on optimism and decreased on tolerance.

APPENDIX TABLE 20

Frequency of Changes on Both Scales for the Representative Sample of Teachers Taking the Course

	Tolerance Scale	
Optimism Scale	Decrease	Increase
Decrease	4	9
Increase	5	5

Cross-correlations were run between all the background variables and the change scores on the two dependent variables. The results of this analysis shed some light on the relationship of background factors to the most frequently noted change pattern (i.e., the decrease in optimism and increase in tolerance).

Place of birth, experience with disadvantaged children, and family social position were the three variables which were associated with the most frequently occurring change; however, place of birth was the only variable in which the relationship, as indicated by the Fisher Exact Probability Test, was significant beyond the .05 level.

Place of Birth

Appendix Table 21 shows the changes on the tolerance and optimism scale for teachers when they were classified according to their place of birth as Californians or outsiders. Californians were much more likely to increase in tolerance as a result of the course and were more likely to decrease in optimism. Outsiders did not exhibit a pattern that would differ from a binomial probability of .50.

APPENDIX TABLE 21

Association Between Place of Birth and the Change in Scale Scores Following Treatment

	Place of Birth	
	California	Elsewhere
Increase in Optimism, Decrease in Tolerance	0	5
Decrease in Optimism, Increase in Tolerance	6	3

Note: Fisher's Exact Test = .03. Kendall's tau B = -0.64.

The interpretation of the change scores for the Californians probably relates to the experience of being educated in California, where one is likely to go to school with Mexican-Americans.

The increase in tolerance of the Californians could be accounted for in part by their recognition of a problem of which they had previously been unaware. They recognized legitimate grievances. In addition, they saw a warmth in the Mexican personality and background which they may not have recognized earlier, due to patterns of avoidance of cross-cultural contact.

A decrease in optimism could be accounted for by the inflated optimism resulting from contact with assimilated and middle class Americans in "middle class" schools where most of the teachers had gone. Familiarization with the problems associated with assimilation of Mexican-Americans would deflate the teacher's optimism and make her more realistic in outlook. She may have learned background information from the course which she had not been aware of while attending middle-class California schools.

BIBLIOGRAPHY

REFERENCES CITED IN THE TEXT

Beals, Alan R. Culture in Process. New York: Holt, Rinehart & Winston, Inc., 1967.

Beals, Ralph. "Acculturation." Anthropology Today, ed. A. L. Kroeber. Chicago: University of Chicago Press, 1953. Pp. 621-641.

Bloom, B.; Davis A.; and Hess, R. Compensatory Education for Cultural Deprivation. New York: Holt, Rinehart & Winston, Inc., 1965.

Broom, Leonard et al. "Acculturation: An Exploratory Formulation." Beyond the Frontier: Social Process and Cultural Change. Edited by Paul Bohannan and Fred Plog. Garden City, N.Y.: Natural History Press, 1967. Pp. 255-286.

Cassidy, Harold. Knowledge, Experience and Action: An Essay on Education. New York: Teachers College Press, 1969.

Coladarci, A. P. "The Relevance of Psychology to Education." in George F. Kneller, ed. Foundations of Education, ch. 12, pp. 380-403. New York: John Wiley & Sons, Inc., 1967.

Davis, Allinson. "Society, the School, and the Cultural Deprived Student." Improving English Skills of Culturally Different Youth. U.S. Department of Health, Education, and Welfare, Office of Education. Washington, D.C.: U.S. Government Printing Office, 1964.

Deutsch, Martin et al. The Disadvantaged Child. New York: Basic Books, Inc., 1967.

Dixon, W. J. BMD Biomedical Computer Programs. University of California Publications in Automatic Computation No. 2. Berkeley, Cal.: University of California Press, 1968.

Fuchs, Estelle. "How Teachers Learn to Help Children Fail: A Case Study of a New Teacher in a New York City Slum School." Transaction, V, 9 (September, 1968), 45-49.

Goldberg, Miriam. "Adapting Teacher Style to Pupil Differences: Teachers for Disadvantaged

Children." Education for the Disadvantaged: A Book of Readings. Edited by A. Harry Passow, Miriam Goldberg, and Abraham J. Tannenbaum. New York: Holt, Rinehart & Winston, Inc., 1967. Pp. 465-483.

Goldstein, Bernard. Low Income Youth in Urban Areas: A Critical Review of the Literature. New York: Holt, Rinehart & Winston, Inc., 1967.

Gray, Susan W. and Klaus, R. A. "Interim Report: Early Training Project." George Peabody College and Murfreesboro, Tenn., 1963. City Schools. Mimeo.

Groff, Patrick J. "Teaching the CD Child: Teacher Turnover." California Journal of Educational Research, XVIII, 2 (March, 1967), Pp. 91-95.

Haubrich, V. F. "Teachers for Big-City Schools." Education in Depressed Areas. Edited by A. Harry Passow. New York: Teachers' College Press, 1963.

Heller, Celia S. Mexican-American Youth: Forgotten Youth at the Crossroads. New York: Random House, Inc., 1966.

Hess, Robert D. "Political Socialization in the Schools." Harvard Educational Review, XXXVIII, 3 (Summer, 1968), 528-536.

Jonnson, Harold A. STEP (San Francisco State College, Sausalito School District, San Francisco Unified School District Teacher Education Project) Final Report, September 1, 1967 to August 31, 1968. Unpublished.

________. "Teaching the Advantaged: An Opinion Survey." Unpublished.

Kimbrough, R. B. Political Power and Educational Decision-Making. Chicago: Rand McNally & Co., 1964.

Lippitt, R. et al. The Dynamics of Planned Change: A Comparative Study of Principles and Techniques. New York: Harcourt, Brace & World, Inc., 1958.

McCloskey, Elinor F. "Urban Disadvantaged Pupils: A Synthesis of 99 Research Reports." Northwest

Regional Educational Laboratory, Portland. Unpublished. (Available from N.R.E.L. in Portland), 1967.

Mehrens, William A., and Ebel, Robert, eds. Principles of Educational and Psychological Measurement: A Book of Selected Readings. Chicago: Rand McNally & Co., 1967.

Report of the National Advisory Commission on Civil Disorders. March, 1968. Otto Kerner, Chairman. U.S. Government Printing Office: 1968 0-291-729. 425 pages.

Ornstein, Allan C. "A Strategy for Preparing and Assisting Teachers of Disadvantaged Youth." Teachers College Journal, XXXIX, 1 (October, 1967), pp. 38-42.

Passow, A. Harry, ed. Education in Depressed Areas. New York: Teachers College Press, 1963.

Ryans, David G. Characteristics of Teachers. Washington, D.C.: American Council on Education, 1960.

Sexton, Patricia Cayo. Education and Income: Inequalities in Our Public Schools. New York: The Viking Press, Inc., 1961.

Siegel, Sidney. Nonparametric Sketches for the Behavioral Sciences. New York: McGraw-Hill Book Co., 1956.

Spindler, G. D. The Transmission of American Culture. Cambridge, Mass.: Harvard University Press, 1959.

Stodolsky, Susan S., and Lesser, Gerald. "Learning Patterns in the Disadvantaged." Harvard Education Review, XXXVII, 4 (Fall, 1967), 546-593.

Taba, Hilda. "Cultural Deprivation as a Factor in School Learning." Causes of Behavior: Readings in Child Development and Educational Psychology. Edited by Judy F. Rosenblith and Wesley Allinsmith. Second edition. Boston: Allyn & Bacon, Inc., 1966.

Trubowitz, Sidney. A Handbook for Teaching in the Ghetto School. Chicago: Quadrangle Books, Inc., 1968.

ADDITIONAL REFERENCES

Adams, Richard N., and Priss, Jack J., eds. Human Organization Research: Field Relations and Techniques. Homewood, Ill.: Society for Applied Anthropology, The Dorsey Press, Inc., 1960.

Becker, Howard S. "Social-Class Variations in the Teacher-Pupil Relationship." Journal of Educational Sociology, XXV, 8 (April, 1952), pp. 451-65.

Bohannan, Paul, and Plog, Fred, eds. Beyond the Frontier: Social Process and Cultural Change. Garden City, N.Y.: Natural History Press, 1967.

Brim, Orville G., Jr. Sociology and the Field of Education. New York: Russell Sage Foundation, 1958.

________, and Wheeler, Stanton. Socialization After Childhood: Two Essays. New York: John Wiley & Sons, Inc., 1966.

Brookover, W. B., and Gotlieb, David. "Social Class and Education." Readings in the Social Psychology of Education. Edited by W. W. Charters, Jr. and N. L. Gage. Boston: Allyn & Bacon, Inc., 1963.

Brown, Roger. Social Psychology. New York: The Free Press, 1965.

Burchill, George W. Work-Study Programs for Alienated Youth: A Casebook. Chicago: Science Research Associates, Inc., 1962.

Bush, Robert N. The Teacher-Pupil Relationship. Englewood Cliffs, N.J.: Prentice-Hall, Inc., 1954.

Charters, W. W., Jr., and Gage, N. L., eds. Readings in the Social Psychology of Education. Boston: Allyn & Bacon, Inc., 1963.

Clark, K. B. Dark Ghetto: Dilemmas of Social Power. New York: Harper & Row, Publishers, 1965.

Coleman, J. S. et al. Equality of Educational Opportunity. Washington, D.C.: U.S. Government Printing Office, 1966.

Corey, Stephen M. Action Research to Improve School Practices. New York: Teachers College Press, 1953.

Foster, George M. Traditional Cultures: and the Impact of Technological Change. New York: Harper & Row, Publishers, 1962.

Frost, Joe L., and Hawkes, Glenn R., eds. The Disadvantaged Child: Issues and Innovations. Boston: Houghton Mifflin Company, 1966.

Ginzberg, Eli, ed. The Negro Challenge to the Business Community. New York: McGraw-Hill Book Co., 1964.

________, and Bray, Douglas W. The Uneducated. New York: Columbia University Press, 1953.

Goodenough, Ward Hunt. Cooperation in Change. New York: Russell Sage Foundation, 1963.

Gordon, Edmund W. "Characteristics of Socially Disadvantaged Children." Review of Educational Research, XXXV, 5 (December, 1965), 377-388.

Gottlieb, D. "Teaching and Students: The Views of Negro and White Teachers." Sociology of Education, XXXVII, 4 (Summer 1964), pp. 345-353.

Gronlund, Norman E. "Relationship Between the Sociometric Status of Pupils and Teachers' Preferences for or Against Having Them in Class." Sociometry, XVI, 2 (May, 1953), pp. 142-150.

Haubrich, V. F. "The Culturally Different: New Context for Teacher Education." Journal of Teacher Education, XIV, 2 (1963), pp. 163-167.

Henry, Jules. "A Cross-Cultural Outline of Education." Current Anthropology, I, 4 (July, 1960), 267-305.

________. Culture Against Man. New York: Vintage Books, 1963.

Hodgkinson, Harold L. Education, Interaction, and Social Change. Englewood Cliffs, N.J.: Prentice-Hall, Inc., 1967.

Hoehn, Arthur J. "A Study of Social Status Differentiation in the Classroom Behavior of Nineteen Third-Grade Teachers." Charters and Gage.

Kaplan, Bert, ed. Studying Personality Cross-Culturally. New York: Harper & Row, Publishers, 1961.

Kroeber, A. L. Anthropology Today. Chicago: University of Chicago Press, 1953.

Lawrence, Paul F. "The Vocational Aspirations of Negro Youth in Secondary Schools of California." Unpublished doctoral dissertation, School of Education, Stanford University, 1948.

Lewis, Hylan. "Culture, Class, and Family Life Among Low-Income Urban Negroes." Employment, Race, and Poverty. Edited by Arthur Ross and Herbert Hill. New York: Harcourt, Brace & World, Inc., 1967.

Lewis, Oscar. "The Culture of Poverty." Scientific American, CCXV, 4 (October, 1966), pp. 19-25.

Liebow, Elliot. Tally's Corner: A Study of Negro Streetcorner Men. Boston: Little, Brown & Co., 1967.

Morris, J. Russell. "The Socio-Economic Background of Negro Migrants to California." Unpublished doctoral dissertation, School of Education, Stanford University, 1947.

Passow, A. Harry; Goldberg, Miriam; and Tannenbaum, Abraham J., eds. Education of the Disadvantaged: A Book of Readings. New York: Holt, Rinehart & Winston, Inc., 1967.

Riessman, F. The Culturally Deprived Child. New York: Harper & Row, Publishers, 1962.

Roberts, Joan I., ed. School Children in the Urban Slum. New York: The Free Press, 1967.

Rocchio, Patrick D., and Kearney, Nolan C. "Teacher-Pupil Attitudes as Related to Nonpromotion of Secondary School Pupils." Charters and Gage.

Roethlisberger, F. Management and Morale. Cambridge, Mass.: Harvard University Press, 1941.

Rosenthal, Robert. Experimenter Effects in Behavioral Research. New York: Appleton-Century-Crofts, Affiliate of Meridith Pub. Co., 1966.

Spindler, George D. Education and Culture: Anthropological Approaches. New York: Holt, Rinehart & Winston, Inc., 1963.

Textor, Robert B., ed. Cultural Frontiers of the Peace Corps. Cambridge, Mass.: The M.I.T. Press, 1966.

Torrance, E. Paul. "Motivating Children with School Problems." Mental Health and Achievement: Increasing Potential and Reducing School Dropout. Edited by E. P. Torrance and R. D. Strom. New York: John Wiley & Sons, Inc., 1965.

Wallace, Anthony F. C. "Culture and Cognition." Science, CXXV, 3501 (February 2, 1962), 351-357.

Wilson, Herbert B. "Evaluation of the Influence of Educational Programs on Mexican-Americans." Unpublished report prepared for the National Conference on Educational Opportunities for Mexican-Americans, April 25-26, 1968, Austin, Texas.

ABOUT THE AUTHOR

ROGER M. BATY is Director, Intercultural Dimension, at Johnson College, University of the Redlands, California. Previously, he served for two years as Director of the Experiment in International Living Independent Study Program in Great Britain and Ireland; he has also taught Peace Corps volunteers and at the elementary school level among the Indians in Montana.

Dr. Baty received his doctorial degree from Stanford University.